TRAVELLERS

NORWAY

By
ZOE ROSS

Written and updated by Zoe Ross
Original photography by Terje Rakke, Nordic Life AS

Published by Thomas Cook Publishing
A division of Thomas Cook Tour Operations Limited.
Company registration no. 1450464 England
The Thomas Cook Business Park, 9 Coningsby Road,
Peterborough PE3 8SB, United Kingdom
E-mail: sales@thomascook.com, Tel: + 44 (0) 1733 416477
www.thomascookpublishing.com

Produced by Cambridge Publishing Management Limited
Burr Elm Court, Main Street, Caldecote CB23 7NU

ISBN: 978-1-84157-898-9

First edition © 2006 Thomas Cook Publishing
This second edition © 2008
Text © Thomas Cook Publishing
Maps © Thomas Cook Publishing/PCGraphics (UK) Limited

Series Editor: Maisie Fitzpatrick
Production/DTP: Steven Collins

Printed and bound in Italy by Printer Trento

Cover photography: Front: Left © Belenos PS/SIME-4Corners Images; Centre
© Cozzi Guido/4Corners Images; Right © Mezzanotte Susy/SIME-4Corners
Images. Back: Left © Belenos PS/SIME-4Corners Images; Right © Borchi
Massimo/4Corners Images

The paper used for this book has been independently certified as having
been sourced from well-managed forests and recycled wood or fibre
according to the rules of the Forest Stewardship Council.
This book has been printed and bound in Italy by Printer Trento S.r.l.,
an FSC certified company for printing books on FSC mixed paper in
compliance with the chain of custody and on products labelling standards.

FSC
Mixed Sources
Product group from well-managed
forests and recycled wood or fibre
Cert no. CQ-COC-000012
www.fsc.org
© 1996 Forest Stewardship Council

Contents

Background	4–25
Introduction	4
The land	6
History	10
Politics	16
Culture	18
Festivals and events	22

First steps	26–9
Impressions	26

Destination guide	30–147
Oslo	30
Day trips from Oslo	44
Bergen	48
Southern Norway	60
The Norwegian fjords	80
Central Norway	102
Northern Norway	124
Svalbard	142

Getting away from it all	148–51

Directory	152–89
Shopping	152
Entertainment	154
Children	158
Sport and leisure	162
Food and drink	166
Hotels and accommodation	172
Practical guide	178

Index	190–91

Maps	
Norway	7
Oslo city map	31
Karl Johans Gate walk	36
Bergen city map	48
Bryggen walk	51
Modern Bergen & Lake Lille Lungegårdsvann walk	52
Southern Norway	60
Central Kristiansand walk	62
Stavanger city	72
The Norwegian fjords	80
The Hardanger Plateau tour	87
Atlantarhavsveien (the Atlantic Road) tour	88
Central Norway	103
The Arctic Circle tour	114
Northern Norway	125
Oslo transport network	186–7

Features	
The Vikings	14
A land of great explorers	46
Norway's national sport	78
Norway's stave churches	98
Norway's trolls & other myths	100
Cod-fishing in the Lofoten Islands	122
Aurora borealis & the Midnight Sun	128
To whale or not to whale?	140

Walks and tours	
Walk: Karl Johans Gate	36
Walk: Bryggen	50
Walk: Modern Bergen & Lake Lille Lungegårdsvann	52
Walk: Central Kristiansand	62
Tour: The Hardanger Plateau	86
Tour: Atlantarhavsveien (the Atlantic Road)	88
Tour: The Arctic Circle	114

Introduction

The magnificent panorama of the fjords, majestic snowy mountains, tranquil lakes and valleys, pine-forested wildernesses; all these and more await the visitor to this country of outstanding natural beauty. No wonder Norway has been one of the main beneficiaries of the recent boom in tourism in Scandinavia. Jutting out into the sea at the northernmost point of Europe, the country has a frontier-like geography that seems reflected in its people: proud, nationalistic and rather isolationist.

The stereotypical images of Norway are of lean, white-blond athletic people, clean, crisp air, snow-covered forests and vast expanses of mountains and waterways stretching into the horizon. All of these are true, but there is much more to the country than the fjords that attract so many crowds every summer or the ski resorts in winter.

Oslo, the nation's capital, is a thriving, glittering city renowned for its world-class museums, youthful glow and buzzing nightlife. Bergen, too, is far more than just a medieval architectural gem; it is also a centre for culture and art, and some of the finest cuisine in the country. The south coast is made up of hundreds of fishing villages and resorts, each with their distinctive character. The north, too, is characterised by its fishing heritage in areas such as the Lofoten Islands, while Tromsø, within the Arctic Circle, is probably the liveliest city this far north in the world. On the border with Finland, the Finnmark region rose from the ashes of World War II and now proudly maintains the heritage and traditions of its Sami people. Then, of course, there are the fjords, the most stunning landscape of its kind anywhere on the planet. No visitor will ever forget the views of shimmering waterways, surrounded by sheer mountain faces, cascading waterfalls and tiny clapboard farming villages, projecting their distinctive red façades on to the lush green fields at the water's edge.

The landscape gives Norwegians more than enough to be proud of, but they are also fierce protectors of their history and heritage. Trolls still feature in the national mind-set as mythical mountain inhabitants who have the ability to aid or hinder the human population according to the manner in which they are treated. The Viking era is carefully preserved in both museums of archaeological discoveries and in the reproduction of Viking jewellery, goblets and helmets that fill souvenir shops the country over. Furthermore, almost every region has at least one open-air museum in which architecture and traditions of days gone by are lovingly restored and preserved. This need to recapture and safeguard the past is possibly due in part to Norway's history of reign by invading nations, but it may also be a way of retaining a national identity while looking to the future and the contentious political question today of whether to join the European Union.

One less palatable stereotype of Norway that is unfortunately true for visitors as well as citizens is the high pricing. Norway is one of the most expensive countries in the world, and a holiday here is likely to have foreigners reeling when they do their accounts at the end of each day. But what you pay for in material goods you more than get back in nature's bounty, and that seems to be a pretty good trade-off for most visitors.

The Seven Sisters Falls at Geiranger

The land

Boasting the northernmost territory of mainland Europe, Norway can also claim the northernmost habitation within the Arctic Circle in its offshore territories of Svalbard and Jan Mayen Island. From the north to the south, this narrow strip of land covers as much as 1,760km (1,094 miles), while its average width is only 200km (124 miles). Given its land area of 323,758sq km (125,004sq miles), Norway is sparsely populated, with a population of around 4.5 million.

From the stark austerity of the icy far north, the landscape transmutes into rolling hills and lush forests in the more temperate areas southwards; the southwest has the most spectacular fjords. The variety and stunning beauty of the landscape offers visitors to Norway a unique experience, and explains why Norwegians themselves have a deep love of the great outdoors.

The coastline and the fjords

A large proportion of life in Norway is influenced by its coastline, which stretches 22,000km (13,670 miles) from the North Sea in the south up to the chilly Arctic Ocean in the north. Inhabitants of these coastal regions and the innumerable offshore islands have, by necessity and skill, survived through fishing and boat-building since ancient times. The sea even encroaches inland, filling the many fjords with water. The fjords were formed following the Ice Ages, when glaciers that once covered the region melted in response to the rising sea level and carved great mountainous valleys on the landscape. The largest fjord is the 200km (124-mile)-long Sognefjord, but hundreds of smaller fjords stretch out like fingers in the southwest. An agricultural region, the coastal area utilises the land to its full potential, primarily by fishing (mainly salmon and trout), goat and sheep farming and the growing of fruit and vegetables.

Mountains and glaciers

The original landscape that was eventually to emerge as the fjords can still be imagined in the surviving glacial areas. Jostedalsbreen, in the west, is the largest glacier region in Europe, with around 26 glaciers. The blindingly white ice packs are a spectacular sight.

The Jotunheimen National Park, in eastern Norway, has some of the country's highest mountains. At 2,469m (8,100ft), Galdhøpiggen is the highest in the country. A close second is nearby Glittertind, which once reached 2,470m

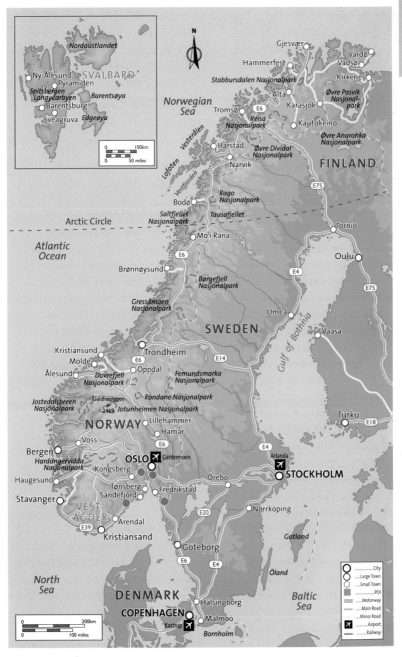

(8,104ft) until its icecap melted and took 7m (23ft) off its height. Where there are mountains there are *fjells* (plateaus), and the largest of these is Hardanger in the south, which is known as the 'garden' of Norway for its fruit and vegetable output.

Forests and tundra

Southern and central Norway are dominated by forests, predominantly pine in the north and deciduous forests in the south, all of which have contributed significantly to the country's timber industry. Through careful management, such as the policy of reseeding following each felling, Norway's forests have survived far better than those of many other countries around the world. Many of the wilderness areas are also now protected as national parks; there are 21 such parks across Norway. The far north has a tundra landscape, a Sami word for the treeless frozen area, dotted only with shrubland, that is their native home.

Climate

More than one-third of Norway lies within the Arctic Circle, but the presence of the Gulf Stream has allowed humans to inhabit this northern stretch more easily than any other part of the world on the same latitude due to the milder climate that this stream brings. It also protects the fishing communities from becoming iced over throughout the year, a fact that has been intrinsic to their livelihood.

Norway's climate often surprises visitors, particularly in summer. In winter, temperatures even in Oslo are just below freezing, but, contrary to popular opinion, summers are pleasant, with an average of 24°C (75°F) in the capital and 18°C (64°F) in northern Tromsø. However, the south in particular suffers from a rain-laden climate, and heavy snow is predictable in winter for the entire country. None of this applies to Norway's northernmost territory Svalbard, where the climate is sub-Arctic.

The distinctive feature of northern Norway's summer months is the phenomenon of sunlight lasting almost 24 hours a day, leading to the country's sobriquet of the 'Land of the Midnight Sun'. In the far north, the sun remains above the horizon for more than 70 days between May and July. The reverse occurs in winter, when the region experiences almost 24 hours of darkness in a day for a certain period. These unique phenomena are caused by the combination of latitudinal position and the slant of the earth's axis as it rotates around the sun.

Flora and fauna

Unsurprisingly, much of the flora of Norway is alpine, with flowers such as forget-me-nots, anemones, sorrel and aster dotting the mountainsides. Wild berries grow in abundance, with blueberries, cranberries and the distinctive cloudberry being the most popular. As well as pine, trees include birch, ash, willow and many others.

The most recognisable animal on the Norwegian landscape is the reindeer, many of which are now semi-domesticated, particularly by the Sami. Brown bears, wolves, wolverines and lynx also inhabit some regions, and are protected by national parks. Husky dogs are a vital commodity in the north, helping to pull dog sledges across the unforgiving ice. Musk oxen became extinct in Norway until they were reintroduced in the 1930s, and now largely live in Dovrefjell National Park (*see pp102–3*). The mountains have populations of lemmings. In the far north, and particularly on Svalbard, the polar bear is ubiquitous. Despite their beauty, these bears pose a very real threat to visitors and inhabitants, and

great care should be taken in these areas. Walruses and seals can be found along the coast, and within the northern ocean waters whales are a regular sight. Smaller animals that make Norway their home include rabbits, beavers, pine martens and deer. The bird commonly associated with Norway is the puffin, but the country has a rich array of other bird life, including guillemots, kittiwakes, petrels, gannets, razorbills and eagles. The country abounds in fish: freshwater species in inland rivers, streams and lakes, and sea fish on the coast. Cod, salmon, trout, herring, halibut and mackerel have all been the mainstays of Norway's highly successful and important fishing industry. Crustaceans such as lobster and crab also thrive here.

The land

A glacier in Nordland

History

c. 7th–5th centuries BC	Hunter-gatherers, as well as the earliest group of Samis, are believed to have settled the land.
780s AD	The Viking voyages begin, with the Norwegian Vikings settling in England, Scotland, Wales, Ireland and as far afield as the Mediterranean and the Middle East.
875	King Harald Hårfagre (Fairhair) unites Norway into a single kingdom, and reigns as its first king.
995	King Olav I Tryggvason converts to Christianity.
997	Trondheim becomes the first capital of the Kingdom of Norway.
1001	Leif Eriksson, son of the Viking Erik the Red, reaches North America, possibly the first European to do so.
1028	King Canute (or Knut) of Denmark conquers Norway, but King Olav II Haraldsson is still supported by Sweden.
1030	King Olav is slain at the Battle of Stiklestad (*see p108*).
1031	King Olav is beatified and his burial place in Trondheim becomes a place of pilgrimage.
1035	King Canute dies and Norway and Denmark sign a treaty according to which the monarchy that produces an heir will take the title of king.
1042	King Magnus of Norway, son of St Olav, ascends the throne.
1047	King Magnus is defeated by his uncle Harald Hårdråde, who allies himself with Denmark.
1066	Harald Hårdråde is killed at Stamford Bridge while attempting to conquer England. He is succeeded by King Olav Kyrre. End of the Viking era.
1184	After several civil wars, the illegitimate King Sverre ascends the throne but is excommunicated by Pope

Innocent III. Bergen becomes the nation's capital.

| 1260 | King Håkon IV Håkonsson establishes a hereditary monarchy. |

1261–2 Norway takes over the governance of Greenland, and then Iceland.

1266 King Magnus VI Lagabøte returns the Isle of Man and the Hebridean islands to Scotland.

1274 King Magnus VI unifies the Norwegian legal system and frees the church from the state.

1308 Oslo becomes the capital.

1319 At the age of three, King Magnus VII Eriksson of Sweden becomes king of Norway and Sweden.

1349 The Black Death bubonic plague, carried across the water from Britain by a trading ship, kills 30 per cent of the population.

1360 The Hanseatic League is established at Bergen, ushering in years of prosperity.

1379 King Håkon VI marries Queen Margarete of Denmark, and their son Olav becomes heir to the thrones of Norway and Denmark.

1397 On the death of her son Olav, Queen Margarete, backing her nephew Erik of Pomerania as king, unites Norway, Denmark and Sweden in the Kalmar Union.

1439 Erik deserts the throne, and Norway falls under Danish rule.

1469 The Orkney and Shetland islands are sold back to Scotland.

1523 Sweden withdraws from the Kalmar Union, leading to its collapse.

1537 Danish becomes the official language of Norway. The Reformation converts the whole of Norway to Protestantism.

1563–70 Seven Years War.

1596 The Dutch explorer Willem Barents discovers the Svalbard archipelago (*see p142*).

1716 Sweden invades Norway, but retreats after the death of King Karl XII at Fredrikstad.

1738–42 The 'Little Ice Age' destroys crops and cattle, causing mass famine.

1807–14 Denmark, and therefore Norway, backs France in the Napoleonic Wars. On Napoleon's defeat, Denmark is forced to give Norway, Iceland and the Faroe Islands to Sweden, but retains Greenland, in the Peace Treaty of Kiel.

1814 A constitution is drawn up on 17 May by parliamentarians of Norway at Eidsvoll (*see p45*). The Swedes accept the constitution within the concept of a joint union, with the Swedish king Karl Johan as monarch.

1825 Norwegians begin a mass emigration to North America that will continue for 100 years.

1850–1900 A 'golden age' of art and culture, with Henrik Ibsen, Edvard Munch, Edvard Grieg and Bjørnstjerne Bjørnson all contributing to the Norwegian cultural scene.

1854 The country's first railway line is laid between Oslo and Eidsvoll.

1905 Norway holds a referendum and gains independence from Sweden. Oslo is again the national capital. Danish prince becomes King Håkon VII of Norway.

1911 Roald Amundsen reaches South Pole (*see pp46–7*).

1913 Norway is one of the first countries in Europe to grant women the right to vote.

1914–18 Norway remains neutral during World War I.

1919–27 Prohibition of alcohol leads to smuggling activities and illegal distillation operations.

1920 Norway joins the League of Nations.

1925 The Svalbard Treaty gives sovereignty over the archipelago to Norway.

1940 Nazi Germany succeeds in occupying Norway and Denmark in June in an operation known as *Weserübung*. King Håkon VII and his government are forced into exile. The Nasjonal Samling (National Socialist Party), led by Vidkun Quisling, forms an interim puppet government with the approval of Adolf Hitler.

1941–5 *Hjemmefronten* (the Norwegian resistance movement) is set up. In 1945 the Germans surrender and leave Norway, but not before razing much of Finnmark to the ground. King Håkon returns from exile, Quisling is executed.

1946 Norway is a founding member of the UN.

1949 Norway joins NATO.

1952 Norway joins the Nordic Council.

1957 Håkon VII dies and is succeeded by King Olav V.

1960 Norway joins EFTA (European Free Trade Association).

1969 Oil deposits are found in the North Sea off the

Norwegian coast, leading to an upsurge in the country's prosperity.

1972 A national referendum is held to determine whether to join the EEC, but the country votes 'no' by a large majority.

1986 Gro Harlem Bruntland becomes Norway's first female prime minister.

1991 King Harald V ascends the throne on the death of his father Olav V.

1994 A second referendum held with regard to joining the EU returns the same verdict, though with a far smaller majority. Lillehammer stages the successful 17th Winter Olympic Games.

2001 Controversy rages when Crown Prince Håkon marries a single mother. Norway is voted the most desirable place to live in the world by the UN.

2005 Arbediderpartiet (*see pp16–17*) regains power.

2008 Stavanger named European City of Culture.

The Vikings

'From the fury of the Norsemen, good Lord preserve us.'

So begins an early English prayer, from the centuries when the Norse raiders in their dragon-headed longships first swept out of the fjords of Scandinavia to harry the coasts of Scotland, Ireland, England and France.

Their name comes from their homeland: *vik* means a narrow inlet off the sea (or a larger fjord), and these fjord-dwelling raiders called themselves *vikingar*. They recognised no ruler except their own chiefs or *jarls*, and worshipped their own fierce gods. Their shallow-draught, square-rigged ships could sail up estuaries or be hauled up on tidal beaches, letting them raid far inland; but they could also navigate huge stretches of open ocean. Vikings from Norway, for instance, attacked the coasts of

Europe as far south as the Mediterranean, settled Iceland, and from there crossed the North Atlantic to Greenland and the shores of North America.

Viking warriors were feared for their ferocity and their skill with axe, sword, spear and bow, and their martial skills commanded a good price in many lands. In the city of Constantinople, capital of the great Byzantine Empire, the emperor's bodyguards were Viking mercenaries known as the Varangir Guard.

In the heyday of the Viking era, Norway was a land held by hundreds of independent *jarls*, each ruling his stretch of fjord and its hinterland with the aid of a household of warriors. But with the coming of Christianity and the rise of feudalism, this independent way of life gradually came to an end, as Norwegian kings extended their control over the *jarls* of the fjords. Many of the more independent-minded Norwegian Vikings resented this, and some left in search of new lands where they could live free of royal interference. In Iceland, the old Viking ways and the old Norse religion lingered long after the pacification of Norway itself.

The carvings on a Viking ship

A ship at the Viking museum, Oslo

The Norse expansion began in the 8th century AD. In AD 793, Viking raiders looted the island monastery of Lindisfarne, off the coast of Northumbria in northeastern England. Within a few years, they were raiding all round the coasts of the British Isles.

Vikings from Denmark headed south into the North Sea, carving out petty kingdoms on the east coast of England and in northern France. Norwegian Vikings took a different track, sweeping westward to settle Orkney and Shetland, and then sailing around the northern tip of Scotland into the Hebrides, where they intermarried with the native Celtic clans to create a unique culture that lasted several centuries. From the Hebrides they moved on to Ireland, where they founded Dublin and other coastal cities.

The era when the Norse warriors swept all before them was brought to an end by a series of decisive battles in which Viking armies were crushed by Irish, English and Scottish kings. The first of these defeats was in 1014 at Clontarf, near Dublin, when Brian Boru, King of Ireland, defeated an army of Vikings from Ireland, Norway and Orkney. Then, in 1066, Harald Hårdråde, King of Norway, in a vain bid for the vacant English throne, led a Viking army to defeat at the hands of the English Earl Harold Godwinsson at Stamford Bridge, in Yorkshire, and the day of the feared warriors of the fjords finally ended.

Politics

After centuries of battles with and invasions from its neighbouring countries, Norway has fiercely tried to preserve a neutral status since it was granted independence in 1905. It may well be this reluctance to take part officially in the machinations of the political world stage that has kept it outside of the European Union for so long, but many believe that the country cannot retain this independent stance forever.

Despite this ongoing debate, however, the most significant aspect of Norwegian politics is its tolerance and support of the people. Religious and political freedom, an excellent record of civil rights and a welfare system that ensures the security of its nationals are the guiding lights of Norwegian governance.

A parliamentary monarchy

The country's 19 *fylkers* (provinces) are governed by a monarchy as well as a parliament (*Storting*) with 169 members. Norway's monarchy is based on the constitution drawn up in 1814 and reinstated after King Håkon's return from exile in 1945. King Harald V (born 1937), of the Glücksberg royal dynasty, has been on the throne since 1991 and is likely to be succeeded by his son, the Crown Prince Håkon, on his death. Despite being vested with certain executive powers, the king's role today is largely ceremonial, with most of his powers handed over to the King's

Council (political cabinet). The king's major role is to serve as a unifying symbol of the country, and the monarchy is deeply loved by the Norwegian people.

The *slattsminister* (prime minister) and members of parliament are elected every four years. The main *Storting*, which is based in the capital Oslo (*see p37*), is divided into two chambers, the Odelsting and the Lagting. While the government officially oversees legislative issues for the whole country, the Sami people (*see p18*) in the north have been granted semi-autonomous rights and have their own parliament to handle regional issues. Most of Norway's industries, including oil and gas, are state-controlled as privatisation is not a concept that has generally entered the Norwegian psyche.

A new beginning

In power in Norway since the 1930s, the Arbediderpartiet (Social Democratic Labour Party) can largely be thanked for the welfare system that has so benefited the country. This party also gave the country its first female prime minister, Gro Harlem Bruntland, in the 1980s. Ousted in the 2001 elections by a coalition of the Kristelig Folkeparti (Christian Democratic Party), the Høyre (Conservative Party) and the Venstre (Liberal Party), they regained power in September 2005 as part of the Red-Green Coalition Party, which swept the polls under the leadership of Jens Stoltenberg.

One of the other features of Norwegian politics is that women play a significant role. Each party is now required by law to have a minimum of 40 per cent female representation as part of an official gender quota.

Economy and welfare

Today, oil is Norway's major source of income, although forestry, fishing, fruit-farming and tourism are also significant contributors to the national economy. It is well known that, although the average earnings of Norwegians far exceed those of the rest of Europe, they are also subject to the highest taxes and the highest prices; a fact that affects every visitor to the country. But so far it has proved a very effective system of putting in to take out. Norway's welfare system is second to none, with free education right up to university level, guaranteed unemployment benefits and pension, free health care and excellent childcare.

The question of the EU

It was in 1972 that Norwegians first voted against membership of the European Union (then the European Economic Community) in a national referendum, based largely on their new-found financial independence after the recent discovery of oil in Norway's North Sea waters. The proposal was rejected again in a second referendum held in 1994. The Norwegian national consciousness is very strong, and many see membership of the EU as a threat to national identity. Many fear, too, that the country's unparalleled social care system will not be sustainable when it comes under the more generalised regulations of the European Union.

However, as more and more nations join the Union, such as the majority of the Eastern European countries in 2004, the question is sure to arise again, particularly if Iceland caves in to pressure and becomes a member. Many worry that Norway is putting itself not in a neutral position, but an isolationist one, which could seriously damage its position within the world economy.

The Norwegian flag

Culture

Norwegians are a fiercely patriotic people, a fact that can be illustrated by their decision on two separate occasions to remain outside the European Union. While much of Norway, whether in the rural or urban sectors, embraces modern technology wholeheartedly, a sense of tradition and history prevails throughout. The country is littered with open-air museums preserving buildings from bygone ages, national costumes are donned on festive holidays, and its three great artistic talents, Henrik Ibsen, Edvard Grieg and Edvard Munch, are celebrated at every turn.

Language

Norway has two official languages: Bokmål and Nynorsk. Spoken by the majority of the population and used as the language of instruction, Bokmål is closely linked with Danish, a remnant of Danish rule over the country for more than 400 years. Nynorsk was invented in the 19th century during a revival in nationalism that would eventually lead to independence. Created by the philologist Ivar Andrea Åsen by drawing on ancient rural dialects, this 'new Norwegian' has closer links with Swedish. While it is the minority language, largely used in the fjord region, a quarter of all television and radio broadcasts are in Nynorsk or subtitled in the language, by government decree.

Dress

In many regions of Norway, traditional clothes were worn every day right up until the 1950s. But today the *bunad* (*see p81*) are only worn during national festivals, such as National Day on 17 May. Traditional costumes are also worn during folk dancing competitions, which are becoming increasingly popular.

THE SAMI

It is thought that the Sami peoples came to Lapland some 4,000 years ago, settling in the northern regions that now lie in Norway, Sweden, Finland and the Kola Peninsula in Russia. The Norwegian Sami population is estimated at around 25,000. Their language is Finn-Ugric in origin, and they traditionally earned their livelihood by reindeer herding and fishing. Many Sami still work at these agricultural activities, although the young are resorting to urban jobs. Tourism is also becoming important to the Sami economy; many settlements accept overnight visitors, and the sale of their distinctive handicrafts is booming. Efforts have been made over the years to assimilate the Sami, but in 1956 a Nordic Sami Council was set up, and they are now officially recognised and their culture preserved. In Karasjok, the Sami even have their own semi-autonomous parliament.

A typical wooden house in the country

Architecture

The common perception of a traditional Norwegian scene is of a red-painted wooden *rorbu*, sitting on the banks of a fjord. These clapboard fishermen's houses are, in fact, prolific all over the country, not just the fjord region. Many of them now act as rural summer houses for city dwellers or as tourist rental properties. Norway's abundance of wood also lent itself to another distinctive form of architecture, that of the medieval stave churches. The few that have survived over the centuries are now protected by conservationists (*see pp98–9*).

The wood-built towns and villages, however, were continually subject to fire hazards, and buildings all over Norway have been forced to rise phoenix-like from the ashes time and

again. For this reason, Oslo is largely constructed in stone, whereas Ålesund's devastation occurred during the trend for Art Nouveau, hence its unique (by Norwegian standards) cityscape in this style (*see p82*). Like much of Europe, Norway was decimated by World War II, and post-war architecture, by necessity, was functional and quickly built. But that is not to say modern architects lack inspiration; a look at the modern museums on Bygdøy (*see pp38–40*) in Oslo, or the Polaria museum in Tromsø (*see p132*) is proof enough of that.

Art

Norway's most famous artist is Edvard Munch (1863–1944) whose *The Scream* is one of the best-known paintings in the world. Munch's art was inspired by

The Beethoven Room in Ringve Musikkhistorisk Museum in Trondheim (*see p109*)

the realist movement, and generally explores psychological themes of the human condition. The other great name on the visual spectrum, and a contemporary of Munch, is Gustav Vigeland (1869–1943). The sculptor's greatest achievement, to which he devoted almost 40 years of his life, is the figures that now stand in Vigeland Park in Oslo (*see p42*). Like Munch, Vigeland was also interested in exploring the human psyche, and the majority of the sculptures explore the cycle of life. Other well-known artists include the 'father of Norwegian painting', Johan Christian Dahl (1788–1857), who is celebrated for his wonderful sweeping landscapes of his native country. Theodor Kittelsen (1857–1914) is known for his

illustrations of trolls and other mythical beings that are so intrinsic to the Norwegian mindset.

Music

If anyone can claim the title of 'national composer', it is Edvard Grieg (1843–1907). Born in Bergen, Grieg derived his inspiration from traditional Norwegian folk music, and his monumental scores of *Peer Gynt* and *Piano Concerto in A Minor* set the majestic Norwegian landscape to music like no other composer before or since. Another musician influenced by folk traditions was the violinist Ole Bull (*see p58*), who travelled the world performing works that had their roots in Hardanger fiddle music. On the opera front, Kirsten Flagstad

(1895–1962) is probably the best-known Norwegian star, earning fame with her performances of Wagner. The popularity of jazz throughout the country, meanwhile, can be seen in the perennially successful Molde Jazz Festival (*see p24*).

Theatre and literature

Without a doubt Henrik Ibsen (1828–1906) is the greatest playwright Norway has ever produced, and statues of the great man are a familiar sight, particularly in Oslo. *A Doll's House* (1880), *The Wild Duck* (1890) and his masterpiece *Hedda Gabler* (1890), which continue to be staged all over the world, are filled with a dark sense of foreboding and, like the work of his contemporaries Munch and Vigeland, involve themselves with the complex issue of human psychology.

Of all the arts, literature in Norway has the longest tradition, emanating from the *Edda*, the Norwegian sagas of the Norse gods. Two Nobel Prize winners for literature made their name by writing about Norwegian peasant life. Bjørnstjerne Bjørnson (*see p33*) and Knut Hamsen (1859–1952) both depicted Norwegian rural life as the very roots of the national consciousness, and their works are now classics.

A statue of Henrik Ibsen stands in front of the theatre where so much of his work was staged

Festivals and events

Whether sport, art, nature or music is your thing, you are bound to find something to suit among Norway's impressive and idiosyncratic calendar of events.

January

Northern Lights Festival, Tromsø

This annual event focuses on the aurora borealis phenomenon as well as concerts and art exhibitions.

Polar Jazz Festival, Svalbard

During the last few days of the month, the northernmost jazz festival in the world shakes up the archipelago of Svalbard.

February

Kristiansund Opera Festival

In the first half of February, the Opera Company stages various productions, while around the town of Kristiansund there are other concerts and art exhibitions.

March

Birkebeiner Race

This 53km (33-mile) cross-country race between Rena and Lillehammer, in which participants have to carry heavy backpacks, takes place in the middle of the month.

Finnmarksløpet, Alta

Europe's longest dog-sledge race occurs in the Finnmark region on 5 March.

Holmenkollen Ski Festival

International ski-jumping competitions are held at the famous ski-jump (*see p42*) just outside Oslo. There is also a cross-country skiing race in which anyone can participate.

Kautokeino & Karasjok Easter Festivals

Norway's two major Sami towns celebrate Easter with reindeer

The Northern Lights

A parade on the streets of Oslo

races and *joik* (chanting) competitions, as well as music and craft activities.

Winter Festival Week, Narvik

Sporting competitions, concerts and parades are the highlights.

World Cod-fishing Championships, Lofoten

Anglers from all over come here to compete for the biggest catch in Svolvær.

April

Voss Jazz Festival

For three days in the first week of the month this famous skiing venue gives itself over to jazz concerts and performances.

May

Bergen International Festival

Probably the most famous cultural festival in the country, this welcomes international performers and musicians. There is a combined focus on contemporary works and those of Grieg and Ibsen.

MaiJazz, Stavanger

The city's oldest festival is also one of the country's best. Well-known Norwegian jazz musicians, as well as international names such as Pat Metheny and Herbie Hancock, have performed here in the past.

Ole Blues Bergen Music Fest

Country and western, blues and folk music.

June

Dragonboat Festival, Bergen

Re-creations of traditional Chinese *drågebats* (dragonboats) are raced by competing teams on the Bergen waterfront.

Festivals and events

Vinstra's Peer Gynt Festival celebrates the famous work by playwright Henrik Ibsen

Norwegian Salmon Festival, Surna

At the end of the month, keen anglers come to Surna to fish in the salmon-rich waters, and various activities, including markets, are based around the country's beloved fish.

Jonsok, 23 June

Bonfires and festivities are held all over the country to celebrate the midnight sun.

North Pole Marathon, Spitsbergen

Billed as 'the world's coolest marathon', this is the northernmost race in the world and probably the toughest marathon across thick ice. Anyone can enter provided they pay the fee.

Viking Festival, Karmøy

Re-creations of Viking battles, Viking crafts and plenty of activities for children bring the past to life for a few days early in the month.

July

Hammerfest Festival

Europe's northernmost town makes the most of the midsummer light with this lively festival.

Molde International Jazz Festival

Jazz musicians from all over the world descend upon this town in the middle of July, with most of the music and action continuing well into the early hours.

Risør Chamber Music Festival

Classical musicians come from all over Norway and the world to perform chamber music concerts for a week.

St Olav Drama and Festival, Stiklestad

The open-air play at the end of July enacting the story of St Olav (*see p108*) is accompanied by a lively festival of medieval activities, such as archery and a medieval market.

August

International Folk Music Festival, Bø

Folk musicians and dancers gather in the town of Bø to celebrate their traditional music.

Norwegian International Film Festival, Haugesund

Norwegian and international films and documentaries are screened in this week-long festival.

Oslo Jazz Festival

An annual event celebrating not only jazz but classical music and dance as well.

Peer Gynt Festival, Vinstra

In honour of Ibsen's famous work, open-air performances of the play are staged in the town of Vinstra. Other highlights include music, exhibitions and parades.

Rauma Rock, Åndalsnes

The country's major rock festival rocks this small town in August. The acts are very Norwegian- or Scandinavian-based.

Varanger Festival, Vadsø

Northern Norway's major jazz festival is held in the middle of the month.

September

Bjørnsonfestivalen, Molde

International literary festival.

International Salmon Fishing Festival, Suldal

The town of Suldal, near Stavanger, is inundated with keen anglers from around the world for this fishing event.

Oslo Marathon

The city's annual 42km (26-mile) run takes place.

October

Osa Festival, Voss

Folk and classical music, as well as lectures and seminars on the history of Norwegian folk music.

December

Nobel Peace Prize Ceremony, Oslo

Every year on 10 December, the announcement of that year's winner of the eminent Peace Prize is made.

Santa Lucia Festival

On the 13th of the month, all over the country young girls dressed in white and carrying candles form a procession in the 'Festival of Lights' to honour the saint.

The Nobel Peace Center, Oslo

Impressions

A trip to Norway constitutes a feel-good experience in all manner of ways. The unpolluted clarity of the air, the vast, beautiful landscapes of mountains and forests, the sense of time and space, the freshness of the food, the efficiency of the services, and the glowing health of the people all contribute to a holiday of relaxation and ease, even if it does come at quite a price.

When to go

For obvious reasons, most visitors come to Norway during the summer months between May and August. The weather is warm (if a little rainy) and, more importantly, there are more daylight hours in which to enjoy yourself; in the south the sun doesn't set until about 11pm, and in the north, the 'land of the midnight sun', you can enjoy sunlight 24 hours a day. Winter visitors tend to be avid ski and snowboard fans, although a chance to see the Northern Lights phenomenon (*see pp128–9*) shouldn't be missed. For other areas, winter should be avoided as many sights are closed or have limited opening hours, and public transport services are usually reduced.

Reindeer are native to Norway

HURTIGRUTEN FERRIES

Since 1893, the Hurtigruten ferries have plied the Norwegian coastline between Bergen and Kirkenes in Finnmark. Originally these began as vital links between communities and a means of transporting goods and communications from one part of the country to another, but today they are very much a tourist link as well. There are 34 ports of call along the route and you can get on and get off wherever you wish, or simply make the full journey for a wonderful view of the changing coastline. The journey from Bergen to Kirkenes takes six days. The ferries provide cabin accommodation for those who are interested, transport cars, and a range of dining options. Timetables are clearly displayed in ferry port offices. *www.hurtigruten.com*

What to do and see

Norway is one of the largest countries in Europe, and unless you have a great deal of time on your hands (and a limitless budget) trying to see the whole place in one trip is pointless. Most first-timers undertake the classic tourist journey from Oslo to Bergen, taking in the spectacular fjord scenery en route. If you are into wildlife-watching, a trip to the north of the country will be worthwhile; whale-watching trips, puffin bird colonies and national parks inhabited by reindeer, elk and brown bear are some of the delights on offer. Norway may not scream sunbathing to most people, but summer in the south is usually warm and sunny, and many of the coastal towns are elegant resorts with yacht harbours and seafood restaurants.

However, be aware that you'll be sharing the sands with innumerable Norwegian holidaymakers. In winter, Lillehammer, Voss and many other resorts offer excellent skiing facilities, while dog-sledging trips in the far north offer an unforgettable experience. Svalbard, off the northern coast, makes for an unusual and exciting trip, but can only really be undertaken as part of an organised tour.

Getting around

Public transport in Norway is excellent and, particularly in the south, no visitor should have any problem getting from one place to another either by bus, train or ferry. Oslo has an extensive Metro and tram network. A few trips, such as

Fields of rape seed flowers in full bloom

The roads in Norway are very good, even in remote places

the Flåm railway in the fjords (*see p94*), have become tourist sights in their own right, while bus journeys offer breathtaking views with the additional benefit of not having to concentrate on the road. Hitchhiking, while not exactly frowned upon, is not a common practice.

Driving

Cars drive on the right-hand side of the road in Norway, so all cars are left-hand drive. Road conditions, particularly in the south, are superb, and some of the more troublesome landscape features, namely lakes and mountains, have been resolved by cutting tunnels through the rock. Longer tunnels are also equipped with fans to remove the threat of fumes. The price to pay for this efficiency, however, is the frequent tollbooth. Note too that in winter months many roads may be closed due to bad weather. While this is unlikely to affect major highways, such as that between Oslo and Bergen, even the fjord region will have certain passes shut off from vehicles.

Speed limits and driving under the influence of alcohol are taken very seriously, and fines are high.

Etiquette

It is generally agreed that Norwegians are a reserved lot, obsessed with politeness and concentrating their social activities into the pursuit of physical wellbeing rather than wild partying. Overall, this can be taken as fact, although the frenetic summer festivals around the country, celebrating a return to daylight, may belie the truth. To outside eyes, Norwegian life may seem rather formal; the handshake, for example, is customary for social situations as well as business. When having a drink with a Norwegian, be sure to wait for them to say '*Skål*' (Cheers) and return the compliment before drinking as it is considered rude to imbibe before this traditional bid to good health. Contrary to popular opinion, Norwegians are not big drinkers and getting drunk in public will be frowned upon.

Language

Norwegians are well aware that theirs is an isolated language and almost all have a good command of English, even in the rural north. Most also have a good knowledge of Swedish and Danish. However, as with travelling in any country, it is always polite to learn a few pleasantries such as 'please' and 'thank you' (*see p183*), if only to acknowledge the fact that you are a visitor in a foreign country.

Norwegian prices

It is almost impossible to take a holiday in Norway on a tight budget. Even Norwegians, with their comparatively high salaries, find prices in their own country dear, and to outsiders the cost of the simplest meal or drink will seem astronomical. Any visitor to the country should factor this into their trip if they are to avoid pecuniary embarrassment, or worse.

Canoeing on a Norwegian lake

Oslo

Norway's capital may not possess the architectural beauty of its neighbours, Stockholm and Copenhagen, but what it lacks in ornamentation it makes up for in its many sights of interest and activities. Museums such as the superb Folk Museum are among Europe's best, while the city's parks offer opportunities for walks and sunbathing in summer and the nearby hills turn into busy ski slopes in winter. This quietly appealing city ensures that those who stop a while to explore its low-key charm will be richly rewarded.

Established by the Vikings in the 11th century and receiving its capital status in the 14th century, Oslo can lay claim to being one of the oldest capital cities in Europe. For several centuries, the city was called Christiania after King Christian IV, who oversaw its rebuilding after it was decimated by fire. However, when Norway gained its freedom from Sweden in 1905 it reverted to the name Oslo in 1924 and became the capital of the new self-governing nation.

Like many of Europe's capital cities, Oslo expanded greatly after World War II when people began to flock from rural areas to find work in the urban sector. Today, one in every four Norwegians lives in Oslo. Despite this, Oslo, which is one of the largest capitals on the continent in terms of area, is also one of the least populated. This is apparent in the leisurely atmosphere of the city and the sense of easy-going life on the wide boulevards – there's none of the bustle and overcrowding that

defines so many urban heartlands. Its location at the head of the Oslofjord also offers a feeling of tranquillity, and many locals are avid sailors, taking to the calm waters for day trips in the summer.

Oslo is the country's centre of art and culture, with works by artists such as Munch and Vigeland taking pride of place. In recent years, it has also shaken off its rather dour image with a new reputation as a nightlife and dining mecca, although visitors may find the prices in one of Europe's most expensive cities take the edge off some of the fun.

CITY CENTRE
Akershus Slott (Akershus Castle)

Looming over the harbour, Oslo's castle and former royal residence was built in 1300, rendering it one of the city's oldest-surviving buildings. The castle is surrounded by a fortress, set up to protect it from waves of invading Swedes. Today, Akershus Castle is

Oslo

primarily used for state ceremonial activities. Visitors can take in the banquet halls, state rooms and dungeons, while the museum within the fortress grounds documents the activities of Norway's Resistance movement during World War II (*see p34*).

Festnings-Plassen. Tel: (47) 23 09 35 33. Open: 2 May–5 Sept Mon–Sat 10am–4pm, Sun 12.30–4pm; 16 Sept–May Thur noon–2pm. Admission charge.

Astrup Fearnley Museet (Astrup Fearnley Museum of Modern Art)

A series of exhibitions, featuring international artists such as Andy Warhol and Damien Hirst, changes every few months in Oslo's major modern art gallery.

Dronningens gate 4. Tel: (47) 22 93 60 60. www.afmuseet.no. Open: Tue, Wed & Fri 11am–5pm, Thur 11am–7pm, Sat & Sun noon–5pm. Closed: Mon. Free admission.

Akershus Castle is one of the oldest-surviving buildings in Oslo

Harbour

The setting for ferries taking
commuters and tourists to
neighbouring islands and out to the
fjords, Oslo's harbourfront is, at most
times of year, more practical than
ornamental. But the views across the
water are stunning, as are those of the
Oslo skyline, and in summer the area
comes alive with markets, concerts and
various festive events.

Historisk Museet (Historical Museum)

On display here are artefacts from the
Viking era and the Middle Ages, including
Viking jewellery and weapons, images of

medieval saints, relics from stave churches
and a numismatic collection of ancient
Norwegian coins. The museum also
hosts temporary exhibitions.
*Fredericks gate 2. Tel: (47) 22 85 99 12.
www.khm.uio.no. Open: mid-May–mid-
Sept Tue–Sun 10am–4pm;
mid-Sept–mid-May Tue–Sun
11am–4pm. Admission charge.*

Ibsen Museet (Ibsen Museum)

Henrik Ibsen's former apartment,
where he spent the last 11 years of his
life and wrote his last play *When We
Dead Awaken* (1899), has now been
turned into a museum. Set up to look
as it would have at the time of Ibsen's

BJØRNSTJERNE BJØRNSON

One of Norway's great men of letters, Bjørnson (1832–1910) is best remembered today for writing the lyrics of the country's National Anthem.

After an idyllic childhood in the Romsdal region, Bjørnson came to Oslo to study at the university and then work as a journalist and drama critic. His first novel, *Synnøve Solbakken*, was the first of four tales to dwell on Norwegian peasantry, and he became inextricably linked with this subject. In 1862, his poetic trilogy, *Sigurd Slembe*, made his name across Europe. Bjørnson focused on politics in later years, taking to heart the travails of his country attempting to free itself from Swedish rule. He wrote the eight verses of the Anthem in 1859–68, evoking the nation's warrior past and also its pastoral present. In 1903, Bjørnson was awarded the Nobel Prize for Literature for his celebration of Norwegian life.

death in 1906, the museum's focal point is the study where Ibsen worked.
Henrik Ibsens gate 26. Tel: (47) 22 55 20 09. www.ibsenmuseet.no. Open: 24 May–15 Sept Tue–Sun 11am–6pm; 16 Sept–24 May Tue–Sun noon–3pm

Kunstindustrimuseet (Museum of Decorative Arts & Design)

Norwegian arts and crafts through the ages, as well as furniture, 18th-century silver items and a medieval tapestry are exhibited here. Fashion aficionados will enjoy the history of fashion design.
*St Olavsgate 1. Tel: (47) 22 03 65 40. www.nasjonalmuseet.no.
Open: Tue–Fri 11am–5pm (until 7pm Thur), Sat & Sun noon–4pm. Admission charge.*

Museet for Samtidskunst (National Museum of Contemporary Art)

Formerly housed in the National Gallery, Norway's post-war contemporary art collection was moved to its own larger exhibition space here in 1990, allowing the bold, modern works to be appreciated in a more expansive setting.
Bankplassen 4. Tel: (47) 22 86 22 10. www.nasjonalmuseet.no. Open: Tue–Wed & Fri 11am–5pm, Thur 11am–7pm, Sat & Sun noon–5pm. Free admission.

Nasjonalgalleriet (National Gallery)

Among the highlights in Norway's National Gallery is Edvard Munch's most famous painting, *The Scream*, as well as exhibitions detailing the history

The National Gallery in Oslo

A view of the City Hall and harbour front

and psychology of this disturbing work. Other Norwegian greats such as J C Dahl and Harriet Backer have areas devoted to their work, as does the famed sculptor Gustav Vigeland. International artists featured here include Cézanne, Matisse, El Greco and van Gogh.

Universitetsgate 13. Tel: (47) 22 20 03 41. www.nasjonalmuseet.no. Open: Tue–Wed & Fri 10am–6pm, Thur 10am–7pm, Sat & Sun 11am–5pm. Admission charge.

Norges Hjemmefrontmuseet (Norway's Resistance Museum)

The history of Norway's resistance against the German Nazi occupiers during World War II is extremely well documented here. Among the exhibits are radio transmitters and secret printing presses used to communicate the activities of the resistance movement. Some of the tales of oppression on record are heart-rending, such as that of a prisoner of war who kept a diary of his ordeal by pricking words onto lavatory paper with a nail. He was eventually murdered, but his diary, discovered after the German surrender, lives on to tell his tale. A monument by the entrance commemorates the brave members of the resistance executed by the Germans on this site.

Akershus Fortress. Tel: (47) 23 09 31 38. Open: Sept–May Mon–Fri 10am–4pm, Sat & Sun 11am–4pm; June–Aug Mon–Sat 10am–5pm, Sun 11am–5pm. Admission charge.

Rådhus (City Hall)

Despite its modern (1950) and, some say, rather ugly design, various nods to

Norway's 900-year history have been incorporated into Oslo's administrative centre, located on the harbour front. Carvings depicting scenes from Norse mythology adorn the façade, while the interior has a fresco entitled *Life* by Edvard Munch, an astronomical clock, and various tapestries and sculptures. The Rådhus is the venue for the Nobel Peace Prize award ceremony in December every year.

Rådhusplassen. Tel: (47) 23 46 16 00. Open: daily May–Aug 8.30am–5pm; Sept–Apr 9am–4pm. Admission charge.

Teatermuseet (Theatre Museum)

Norway's national playwright, Henrik Ibsen, naturally dominates the city's theatre museum, but it also houses plenty of other pieces of theatrical memorabilia. There are also recordings of great performances of the past, including those of the internationally acclaimed Norwegian opera singer, Kirsten Flagstad. The museum is set in the former town hall, which was the scene of the first theatrical performance in the city in 1667.

Christiania Torv 1. Tel: (47) 22 42 65 09. www.teatermuseet.no. Open: Thur & Sun noon–4pm, Wed 11am–3pm. Admission charge.

Vår Frelsers Gravlund (Our Saviour's Cemetery)

This graveyard in the city centre is the burial ground for Norway's three greatest cultural icons, Henrik Ibsen, Edvard Munch and Bjørnstjerne Bjørnson. Ibsen's tomb is marked with an obelisk and a hammer, and Bjørnson's by a stone replica of the Norwegian flag in honour of his having written the national anthem. Munch, who died and was buried at the height of the country's occupation by Nazi Germany, has no such grand memorial. *Akersbakken.*

The Theatre Museum in Oslo

Walk: Karl Johans Gate

The city centre's primary thoroughfare, Karl Johans Gate cuts a slice down Oslo's heart from the cathedral to the royal palace. A stroll along the route will take in many of the capital's most significant buildings, and on a summer's day the park areas make for pleasant picnic spots.

Allow half a day.

Start at the corner of Stortorvet and Møllergata.

1 Oslo Domkirke (Oslo Cathedral)

Located in the city's former marketplace, the grandiose cathedral dates from the 17th century but was renovated in the mid-20th century. Among its original architectural features are the pulpit and the altar. Of particular note are the stained-glass windows, designed by Emanuel Vigeland, brother of the great sculptor Gustav Vigeland.

At the eastern end of Stortorvet turn right into Kirkegata and then left into Tollbugata.

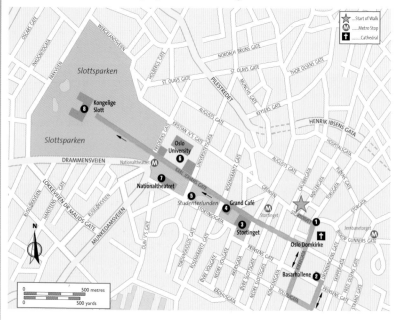

2 Basarhallene (Bazaar Halls)

Behind the cathedral, these cavernous halls are the setting for a handicrafts market during the summer months.
Retrace your steps to the Domkirke and turn left on to Karl Johans Gate. Follow the road for 500m (547 yds).

3 Stortinget (Parliament Building)

Built in 1866, the round, yellow-bricked neo-Romanesque Norwegian Parliament building houses the Norwegian government's sittings every year from October to the middle of June.
Continue walking westwards along Karl Johans Gate for all the sights described here.

4 Grand Café

Set within the equally prestigious Grand Hotel, Norway's most famous café earned its reputation as the daily haunt of Ibsen, and subsequent Norwegian illuminati. On the back wall is a mural depicting Ibsen, Munch and the poet Bjørnstjerne Bjørnson.

5 Studenterlunden

With its proximity to the university, this small patch of parkland is often filled with students, hence its name. In winter, when the pond freezes over, it turns into a popular open-air ice rink.

6 Oslo University

The main draw for tourists in the city's main university building, completed in 1852, is the Aula, the Assembly Hall, which is decorated with three frescoes by Edvard Munch, entitled *Sun*, *Alma Mater* and *History*.

7 Nationaltheatret (National Theatre)

A statue of Norway's greatest dramatist, Henrik Ibsen, graces the entrance to the National Theatre, which is a fitting tribute given that the theatre was constructed to stage his work and many of his now internationally famous plays were premiered here.

8 Kongelige Slott (Royal Palace)

Completed in 1848, Norway's main royal residence is closed to the public. The highlight here is Constitution Day (17 May) when the royal family appears and a marching band plays.

Oslo Domkirke (Oslo Cathedral)
Stortorvet 1. Tel: (47) 23 31 46 00.
Closed for renovation.
Stortinget (Parliament Building)
Karl Johans Gate 22. Tel: (47) 23 31 35 96. www.stortinget.no. Tours available mid-June–Aug Mon–Fri 10am, 11.30am & 1pm; Sept–mid-June Sat & Sun 10am, 11.30am & 1pm. Admission charge.
Grand Café
Karl Johans Gate 31. Tel: (47) 23 21 20 00. www.grand.no. Open: 6.30am–midnight.
Oslo University
Tel: (47) 22 85 95 55. www.uio.no. Open: mid-June–mid-Aug daily 10am–3pm.
Nationaltheatret (National Theatre)
Johanne Dybwads Plass 1. Tel: (47) 22 00 14 00. www.nationaltheatret.no
Kongelige Slott (Royal Palace)
Drammensveien 1. Tel: (47) 22 04 87 00. www.kongehuset.no

BYGDØY

Southwest of the city centre, the well-forested Bygdøy Peninsula attracts tourists with its plethora of world-class museums. It is also a relaxed beach area in summer. A ferry from the harbour opposite the Rådhus carries visitors to Bygdøy daily during the summer, and the peninsula is serviced by a well-run network of buses that stop at each of the museums. There is also a bus from Karl Johans Gate to the peninsula, but this is a much longer journey.

Frammuseet (the polar ship *Fram*)

The polar ship *Fram*, which carried both Fridtjof Nansen to the North Pole and Roald Amundsen to the South Pole (*see pp46–7*), is the *raison d'être* of this museum, and children in particular will relish the opportunity to climb aboard the ship itself. The rest of the museum documents the history and all the dangers, hardships and triumphs of polar expeditions in the 19th and 20th centuries. There is also a section devoted to polar wildlife, including a re-created icecap filled with squealing penguins.
Bygdøynesveien 36. Tel: (47) 23 28 29 50. www.fram.museum.no. Open: daily May–Sept 10am–5pm; June–Aug 9am–6pm; Oct–Feb 10am–3pm; Mar–Apr 10am–4pm. Admission charge.

Kon-Tiki Museet (Kon-Tiki Museum)

The explorer Thor Heyerdahl (*see pp46–7*) was fascinated with the idea of re-creating a raft built from balsa wood as in ancient times. Naming it the *Kon-Tiki*, he and his crew sailed it from Peru to Polynesia in 1947. The raft is now housed at the Kon-Tiki Museum, where visitors can also marvel at the flimsy papyrus *Ra II* raft, based on an ancient Bolivian design, on which Heyerdahl sailed across the Atlantic in 1970.
Bygdøynesveien 36. Tel: (47) 23 08 67 67. www.kon-tiki.no. Open: daily Apr–May & Sept 10am–5pm; June–Aug 9.30am–5.30pm; Oct, Mar 10.30am–4pm; Nov–Feb 10.30am–3.30pm. Admission charge.

Norsk Folkemuseum (Norwegian Folk Museum)

As the museum proudly boasts, 'come here and see Norway in a day'. Visitors can easily pass a whole day in this extensive and fascinating open-air museum exploring the history of the country through 140 relocated preserved buildings, wildlife areas, cooking and craft displays, and more. You can buy sweets and condiments at the village shop, set up to look like a turn-of-the-20th-century store, take a buggy ride through the 'rural' landscape of timber houses and a stave church, eat a piece of freshly baked and buttered *lefse* (the traditional bread), and learn the history of Norwegian folk costumes and Sami traditions. Of particular interest is a re-created tenement flat that has been duplicated to show

how it would have looked in the 1870s and again in the 1970s.

Museumsveien 10. Tel: (47) 22 12 37 77. www.norskfolkemuseum.no. Open: Jan–mid-May Mon–Fri 11am–5pm, Sat & Sun 11am–4pm; mid-May–mid-Sept daily 10am–6pm; mid-Sept–Dec Mon–Fri 11am–3pm, Sat & Sun 11am–4pm. Admission charge.

Norsk Sjøfartsmuseum (Norwegian Maritime Museum)

Norway's oldest-surviving boat, dating from the 2nd century BC, is one of the many exhibits at a museum that documents the country's dependence on maritime activity, both exploration and as a survival necessity through fishing and fish-farming. Other displays

Oslo

The Frammuseet commemorates the polar ship *Fram*

The City Museum in Oslo

include artefacts from various voyages through the centuries, as well as maritime paintings and videos. The ship *Gjoa*, sailed by Roald Amundsen, is stationed at the museum's entrance.

Bygdøynesveien 37. Tel: (47) 24 11 41 50. www.norsk-sjofartsmuseum.no. Open: daily, mid-May–Aug 10am–6pm, Sept–mid-May 10.30am–4pm except Thur 10.30am–6pm. Admission charge.

Vikingskiphuset (Viking Ship Museum)

Three remarkable Viking ships, the *Oseberg,* the *Gokstad* and the *Tune*, are on display at the city's most acclaimed museum. Uncovered in the waters of the Oslofjord near Tonsberg, these spectacular ships, with their sheer size and intricacy of construction, bear witness to the Vikings' seafaring abilities. The *Oseberg* is the most impressive, with its dragonhead carvings, burial chamber and space for around 30 oarsmen. The ships are the true stars of the show and deserve the most attention, but there are also plenty of items of jewellery, weaponry, textiles and tools to entrance anyone interested in this period of Norse history.

Huk Aveny 35. Tel: (47) 22 13 52 80. www.ukm.uio.no. Open: May–Sept 9am–6pm; Oct–Apr 11am–4pm. Admission charge.

AROUND THE CITY CENTRE
Damstredet

In what is otherwise a fairly dull and unenticing area, this section of sloping wooden houses has a certain charm. Most of the houses are occupied by artists.

Frognerparken (Frogner Park)

Located northwest of the city centre, this is one of Oslo's most popular parks, with idyllic pathways, ponds and streams. In summer, the park is a popular picnic area. Frogner Park also draws visitors to its eclectic museums and Vigeland sculptures.

Oslo Bymuseum (Oslo City Museum)

A 1,000-year trawl through the history of the city can be explored at Oslo's official museum in the Vigeland Park area. Models of how the city once looked, as well as paintings and photographs, provide a picture of its changing landscape, while in Frogner Manor interior furnishings are displayed as they would have been in the 18th and 19th centuries.
Frognerveien 67. Tel: (47) 23 28 41 70. www.oslobymuseum.no.
Open: Sept–May Tue–Fri 10am–4pm, Sat & Sun 11am–4pm; June–Aug Tue–Fri 10am–6pm, Sat & Sun 11am–5pm. Admission charge, free Sat.

Skøytemuseet (Ice Skating Museum)

Figure skating and speed skating are two aspects of the same sport, and both are much loved by Norwegians. The skating museum devotes itself to the history and techniques of both, and the many champions the country has produced. A large portion of the museum is given over to the story of Sonja Henie, the 1930s Olympic champion who became, for a short time, a Hollywood star.
Frogner Stadium, Middelthunsgate 26. Tel: (47) 22 43 49 20. Open: Tue & Thur 10am–2pm, Sun 11am–2pm. Admission charge.

Vigeland-museet (The Vigeland Museum)

The largest collection of work by Norway's most acclaimed sculptor Gustav Vigeland (*see p20*) under one roof, the museum includes sculpted studies in plaster, preliminary sketches and woodcarvings. The life and work of Vigeland is also documented here.

A sculpture by Gustav Vigeland outside the Vigeland Museum

Nobelsgate 32. Tel: (47) 23 49 37 00.
www.vigeland.museum.no.
Open: June–Aug Tue–Sun 11am–5pm;
Sept–May Tue–Sun noon–4pm.
Admission charge (free Oct–Mar).

Vigelandsparken (Vigeland Park)

Gustav Vigeland fulfilled his life's
achievement in the creation of this
park, which contains more than 200
examples of his work. The most famous
piece is the *Vigeland Monolith*, a
14m (46ft)-high composition of 121
figures carved out of one piece of stone
and intended to depict life in all its
guises. A path leads past all the other
works, including the flowing, circular
sculpture *Wheel of Life*, which
continues the theme of the cycle
of life.
Nobelsgate 32. Open: daily.
Free admission.

Grønland

Norway is not generally known for
being multiracial, with immigration
rules being among the strictest in
Europe, but the ethnic communities
that do reside in the capital generally
make their home in the Grønland
district, east of the Central Station.
The area is also popular, therefore,
with Oslovians for its many budget-
priced (by Norwegian standards)
ethnic restaurants. An unusual sight
here is the stone fist clutching a rose
that reaches out from the pavement,
a sculpture intended to promote
harmony among nations.

Holmenkollen Skimuseet (Holmenkollen Ski Museum)

The spectacular ski jump that
dominates the Oslo skyline in the
northwest of the city dates back to
1892. A ride in the lift to the top of the
jump not only offers panoramic views
but also gives some idea of the skill and
bravery of trained ski-jumpers. If you
want to experience the thrill for
yourself, there is a simulator that will
have you feeling like you are soaring
through the air.

Every year in March the annual ski-
jumping festival is held here (*see p22*).
At the ski jump's base is a museum that
documents the history of skiing
through the ages, as well as the polar
expeditions undertaken by Amundsen
and Nansen (*see pp46–7*). The sledge-
cum-boat that Nansen used on his
Greenland expedition is on display here.

Just north of the ski jump is the
Tryvannstårnet observation tower that
offers even better views of the Oslofjord.
Kongeveien 5. Tel: (47) 91 67 19 47.
www.holmenkollen.com. Open: June–July
daily 9am–8pm; Aug–Sept & May
10am–5pm; Oct–Apr 10am–4pm.
Admission charge.

Tøyen

Botanisk Hage (Botanical Gardens)

Palm trees, cacti and other exotic
plants, as well as a vast selection of
alpine plants, all find their home here.
Greenhouses are the setting for tropical
plants, while a variety of perennials is
housed in the arboretum. There's also

Vigeland Park

an area known as the Economic Garden, which focuses on plants that have an economic value. The gardens are owned and cared for by the University of Oslo.

Sars Gate 1. Tel: (47) 22 85 16 30.
Open: Apr–Sept Mon–Fri 7am–8pm, Sat & Sun 10am–8pm; Oct–Mar Mon–Fri 7am–5pm, Sat & Sun 10am–5pm.
Free admission.

Munch-Museet
(The Munch Museum)
More than 1,000 paintings by Norway's most acclaimed artist are on display in a museum devoted entirely to his work. Highlights include the picture *The Sick Child*. There are also sculptures, prints and early sketches, all giving an insight into the artist's motivation and development of style throughout his career.

Tøyengate 53. Tel: (47) 23 49 35 00.
www.munch.museum.no.
Open: June–Aug daily 10am–6pm;
Sept & May Tue–Fri 10am–4pm,
Sat & Sun 11am–5pm.
Admission charge.

Day trips from Oslo

Oslo provides a good base from which to see sights and attractions outside the city, giving a taste of the Norway beyond the capital.

Åmot i Modum

This small town 70km (43 miles) south of Oslo earned fame for its cobalt mines, and today makes a popular day trip from the capital (*www.blaa.no*).

Cobalt mines

Visitors are given a helmet and jacket before being led down into the tunnels and quarries of the former cobalt mines, an experience that gives far more meaning to the dangerous and sometimes terrifying conditions the miners were forced to endure than the exhibits in the small museum on the site. During the 1830s, this was the biggest mining site in the country, with more than 2,000 employees. The three schools set up for the children of the miners are now part of the museum.
Tel: (47) 32 78 67 00.
Open: mid-June–mid-Aug daily 11am–6pm; mid-Aug–mid-June Sat 11am–5pm, Sun 11am–6pm. Free admission.

Haugfoss

The highest waterfall in the area can be appreciated from a specially constructed viewing area where there is a pleasant little café. Another charming aspect of the region is the series of 300-year-old general stores, where you can buy old-fashioned sweets, traditional utensils and much more.
Tel: (47) 32 78 67 00.
Open: mid-May–mid-June & mid-Aug–mid-Sept Tue–Sat 11am–5pm; mid-June–mid-Aug daily 11am–6pm. Free admission.

Royal Blåfarveværk

The former mining community has now been turned into an open-air museum, with various exhibitions detailing the history of the mines and the uses of cobalt. The glassworks area is the most popular, with numerous decorative pieces tinted with the deep blue pigment.
Tel: (47) 32 78 67 00.
Open: mid-May–mid-June & mid-

*Aug–mid-Sept Tue–Sat 10am–5pm;
mid–June–mid-Aug daily 10am–6pm.
Free admission.*

Theodor Kittelsen Museum

The artist Theodor Kittelsen is best
known in Norway for his paintings of
trolls and other mythical creatures in
oil or watercolours and woodcarvings.
Much of his work has been gathered
together in this small museum.
Tel: (47) 32 78 67 00.
*Open: mid-June–mid-Aug daily 11am–
6pm; mid-Aug–mid-June Sat 11am–
5pm, Sun 11am–6pm. Admission charge.*

Eidsvoll

Norway's constitution was written
during a six-week period in 1814 in the
19th-century manor house of Eidsvoll,
70km (43 miles) from Oslo along
Highway E6. The wooden benches on
which the parliamentarians sat to draft
the paper can still be seen here, while the
rest of the house has been preserved as it
was when the aristocratic Ankers family
lived here. Their antique furniture and
cast-iron stoves can still be seen.
*Carsten Ankers vei 19. Tel: (47) 63 92 22
10. www.eidsvoll1814.museum.no.
Open: mid-June–mid-Aug daily
10am–5pm; mid-May–mid-June & mid-
Aug–mid-Sept daily 10am–3pm; mid-
Sept–mid-May Sat & Sun 11am–2pm.
Admission charge.*

Hadeland Glassverk, Jevnaker

A trip to these historic glassworks, set
up in 1762, is a great day out for the
whole family. Glass-blowing seems like
an impossible task to all but the
trained, and most visitors watch in awe
as the craftsmen miraculously turn red-
hot bubbles into intricate vases and
other glass objects. Children are
welcome to try their hand at blowing,
or can dye their own candles in the
wax section.
*60km (37 miles) from Oslo on Route 241.
Tel: (47) 61 31 66 00. Open: Mon–Fri
11am–4pm, Sat 10am–4pm, Sun
11am–5pm. Free admission.*

Vikinglandet (Viking Land)

Located 10km (6 miles) south of the
city centre, this theme park will delight
children of all ages, with its
reconstructed houses, boats and
Viking-themed food. The Viking voyage
simulates an 'authentic' trip, complete
with storms and attacks. Added
attractions are a roller coaster, a merry-
go-round and stage performances.
*Vinterbro. Tel: (47) 64 94 63 63.
Open: June–mid-Aug daily 1–7pm.
Admission charge.*

Hand-blown glass on display

A land of great explorers

Perhaps it is the country's isolation at the northern tip of the world, or its proximity to the largely uncharted Arctic Zone that has given Norway a long-standing tradition of intrepid and brave explorers. Even in the Viking era, there was a restless need to expand boundaries, and Norsemen are believed to have reached as far as North America, 400 years before Columbus claimed the discovery as his own. Norway's three most famous sons who devoted their lives to the exploration of new lands are Fridtjof Nansen, Roald Amundsen and Thor Heyerdahl.

Nansen (1861–1930) showed the way, with his crossing of the entire Greenland icefield on skis in 1888, accompanied by five other explorers. His published account of the trip in 1890 not only made him a national hero but also greatly increased the popularity of cross-country skiing (see pp78–9). In 1893, he set off again on a three-year trip aboard the ship *Fram* to the Arctic, continuing across the ice on foot towards the North Pole. Although he didn't reach the Pole itself, he did reach the northernmost point ever seen by man at that time. On his return he conducted groundbreaking research, in his role as an oceanographer, into the nature of ocean currents. Following Norwegian independence, Nansen turned his attention towards politics and became an Ambassador and then a High Commissioner with the newly established League of Nations. It was in the latter role that he won the Nobel Peace Prize in 1922 for his work in assisting refugees created in the aftermath of World War I.

Greatly inspired by Nansen's journeys, Roald Amundsen (1872–1928) determined to spend his life in pursuit of both the North and South Poles. In 1903, aboard the ship *Gjøa*, he became the first to sail through the Northwest Passage between the Atlantic and the Pacific, a route that had eluded many previous explorers for centuries, and charted much of Canada's icy north. His next intention was to reach the North Pole, but he discovered just in time that two other explorers had preceded him. So in 1910, sailing in his hero's ship, the *Fram*, he secretly went the opposite way, heading off for the South Pole. He and his crew were in a fierce race against time with his competitor Captain Scott. By October 1911, using the invaluable dog-sledging skills Amundsen had learned from locals in Canada, the team left the *Fram* and began the drive to the Pole, being the first to reach it on 14 December. Scott reached the Pole a mere 35 days later, but was tragically never to return from the trip. Then, in 1926, Amundsen and an Italian called Umberto Nobile made the first ever successful crossing of the Arctic in the airship *Norge*, flying from Svalbard to Alaska. All other accounts of having reached the North Pole had, by this time, been disputed, so Amundsen could claim to be the first man to reach both Poles after all. Two years later Nobile set off on a repeat trip but went missing, and Amundsen went in search of his friend. He, too, was never seen again; his plane was discovered weeks later near Tromsø.

The 20th century saw yet another great Norwegian explorer, but this time the focus of interest was not the icy regions of the Arctic and the Antarctic but the vast oceans of the Pacific and Atlantic. Thor Heyerdahl (1914–2002) was primarily an anthropologist, fascinated with the possibility that ancient civilisations could have followed a different settlement path than those originally thought. In 1947, Heyerdahl and his crew travelled to South America where they built a raft, the *Kon-Tiki*, made out of balsa wood and based on ancient Inca designs. They sailed the raft 6,920km (4,300 miles) from Peru to Polynesia in just over three months. Heyerdahl's mission was to prove that it was possible for the Polynesian islands to have been settled by South Americans centuries before. Almost 25 years later, he once again built two rafts, the *Ra* and *Ra II*, this time out of papyrus, and sailed from Morocco to Central America. This time he was intent on proving that the Ancient Egyptians could very easily have migrated to the Americas, giving some basis to the argument that the Mexican temples were inspired by the pyramids. Pyramidal structures engaged him in other areas of the world too. In the Maldives and the Canary Islands he ascertained that such structures centring on astronomical factors could clearly have been the result of migration between the Indian Ocean, the Mediterranean and the Americas. In truth, few of Heyerdahl's assertions have ever been taken very seriously by more academic historians and archaeologists, but his flamboyant character and reckless bravery on the ocean waves remain an inspiration for many Norwegians.

Bergen

Bergen may be Norway's second city, but many Norwegians consider it to be the true capital of the country, partly because it has been allowed to retain its historic character and beauty, without any of the administrative modernity that has been forced upon Oslo. Many visitors never realise quite how large the city and its environs are, largely due to its picturesque setting.

For many, Bergen consists purely of its harbourside quadrant, scenically reflected in the waters of the Vågen. Known as the 'gateway to the fjords', the city is an urban jewel in which visitors can spend a few days profitably before sailing off into the water wonderland of Norway's lakes and mountains.

Bergen

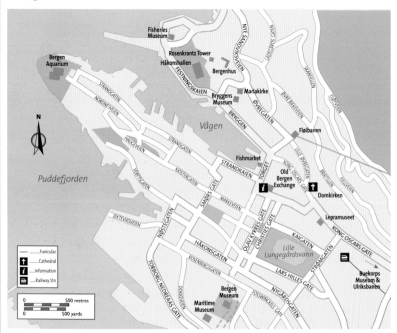

OLD BERGEN
Domkirken

Bergen's cathedral dates from the 12th century, when it was dedicated to St Olav, but many renovations and changes have been made to it over the centuries, largely due to fires that have always been a threat to Bergen's landscape. The Gothic choir is original, as indeed is the dent from a cannonball that was fired at the church in the 17th century.

Kong Oscars gate. Tel: (47) 55 31 58 75. Open: mid-June–Aug Mon–Sat 11am–4pm; Sept–mid-June Tue–Fri 11am–12.30pm. Free admission.

Håkonshallen (Håkon's Hall)

Built in the 13th century by King Håkon Håkonsson for the occasion of the wedding and coronation of his son Magnus Lagabøte, this was the largest royal residence in the country at the time. Bergen was then the political capital of Norway. Like much of Bergen the hall was severely damaged during the explosion of a German ammunition ship during World War II, but it was restored after the war.

Bergenhus. Tel: (47) 55 58 80 10. Open: mid-May–Aug daily 10am–4pm; Sept–mid-May noon–3pm except Thur 3–6pm. Admission charge.

Old Bergen Exchange

What was once the Bergen Exchange now houses a large tourist information centre and includes the Fresco Hall, built in 1862. The frescoes, painted in the 1920s by the artist Axel Revold, take up three themes of Norwegian life. The North Country Wall illustrates life in the Lofoten Islands and their dependence on the fishing industry, the Bergen Wall concentrates on the importance of shipping in the city, and the World Wall deals with the Industrial Revolution. Most visitors will come to the tourist office at some point in their stay; be sure not to miss these murals.

Vågasllmenningen 1. Tel: (47) 55 55 20 00. Open: June–Aug daily 8.30am–10pm; May & Sept daily 9am–8pm; Oct–Apr Mon–Sat 9am–4pm. Free admission.

Rosenkrantztårnet (Rosenkrantz Tower)

In the 1560s, Erik Rosenkrantz, the governor of Bergenhus (Bergen Castle), built this tower partly as a residence and partly as a defence measure. Earlier defence structures that occupied the site were incorporated into the design. Today, the tower is a museum illustrating both the history of the city and its military and defence heritage. Those with a head for heights can climb the narrow spiral staircase to the top of the tower for wonderful views of the Old Town.

Bergenhus. Tel: (47) 55 31 43 80. Open: daily mid-May–Aug 10am–4pm; Sept–mid-May noon–3pm. Admission charge.

Walk: Bryggen

Bergen's wharf was a bustling area of trade from the Middle Ages up to the 18th century. That sense of history has never left, thanks to the preservation of many of the former offices and warehouses.

Allow half a day for an exploration of the Bryggen area, but note that the Mariakirken is closed mid-afternoon.

Start your walk on the corner of Bryggens Torget and Nikolaikirkealmenningen.

1 Alleyways

The most atmospheric part of any visit to this area is to wander through its dark narrow alleyways, where balconies overhang and walls lean unevenly.
Walk along the harbour (Bryggen), turn right into Sandbrogaten, right again onto Øvre Dreggsallmenningen and follow the road around to the right.

2 Bryggens Museum

The finds of a series of archaeologists' excavations of the Bryggen area are now displayed here.

3 Bryggen Meeting Point

Known as the Bryggen Meeting Point, the Bryggens Museum entrance is often where guided walks begin.

Bryggens Museum
Dreggsalmenningen 3. Tel: (47) 55 58 80 10. www.uib.no/bmu. Open: May–Aug daily 10am–5pm; Sept–Apr Mon–Fri 11am–3pm, Sat noon–3pm, Sun noon–4pm. Admission charge.

Bryggen Meeting Point
www.bergenguideservice.no

Mariakirken (St Mary's Church)
Dreggsalmenningen. Tel: (47) 55 31 59 60. Open: mid-June–mid-Aug Mon–Fri 9.30–11.30am & 1–4pm; mid-Aug–mid-June Tue–Fri 11am–12.30pm. Admission charge from mid-May–Aug, free rest of the year.

Det Hanseatiske Museum (Hanseatic Museum)
Finnegårdsgaten 1A. Tel: (47) 55 54 46 90. www.hanseatisk.museum.no. Open: mid-May–mid-Sept daily 9am–5pm; mid-Sept–mid-May Tue–Sat 11am–2pm, Sun 11am–4pm. Admission charge.

Schøtstuene (Hanseatic Assembly Rooms)
Øvregaten 50. Tel: (47) 55 31 60 20. www.hanseatisk.museum.no. Open: June–Aug daily 10am–5pm; May & Sept daily 11am–2pm; Oct–Dec & Mar–Apr Sun 11am–2pm. Admission charge.

Galleri Bryggen (Bryggen Gallery)
Svensgården. Tel: (47) 55 31 41 06. www.galleribryggen.no. Open: mid-May–mid-Sept daily 10am–10pm; mid-Sept–mid-May daily 10am–6pm. Free admission.

Theta Museum
Enhjørningsgården. Open: mid-May–mid-Sept Tue, Sat & Sun 2–4pm. Admission charge.

Continue back north along Dreggsalmenningen.

4 Mariakirken (St Mary's Church)

This was the central church of the Hanseatic merchants from 1408 to 1766.

Walk north to the top of the road and turn right into Øvregaten.

5 Det Hanseatiske Museum (Hanseatic Museum)

The best-preserved building in the area has early 18th-century furnishings.

Continue along Øvregaten and turn right on to Finnegardsgaten.

6 Schøtstuene (Hanseatic Assembly Rooms)

Hanseatic merchants of Bergen would have met in these assembly rooms.

Walk south back to Bryggen and turn right. Take the second right into Nikolaikirkealmenningen, then left into Holmedalsgården.

7 Galleri Bryggen (Bryggen Gallery)

Viking reconstructions and contemporary Norwegian arts and crafts.

Return onto Nikolaikirkealmenningen and head north, taking the second left onto Bryggestredet. Turn left onto Enhjørningsgården.

8 Theta Museum

This tiny museum is set in the confined Bryggen building in which the Norwegian resistance movement operated during World War II.

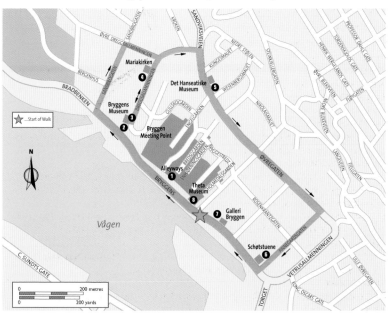

Walk: Modern Bergen & Lake Lille Lungegårdsvann

At the heart of modern Bergen is the attractive Lake Lille Lungegårdsvann, an area that has now been given over to the city's fine collection of art galleries.

Allow half a day to one day, depending on how long you spend inside museums. The walk itself takes just half an hour.

This walk follows a clockwise direction along Rasmus Meyers allé, covering the three sites that together form the Bergen Art Museum (Kunstmuseum): the Lysverket, the Rasmus Meyer Collection and the Stenersen; all three have the same opening hours and contact details.

Start at the eastern shore of Lille Lungegårdsvann.

1 Lille Lungegårdsvann

The lakeside is a pleasant area to start the walk. You can also stop for a rest here at any point to watch the

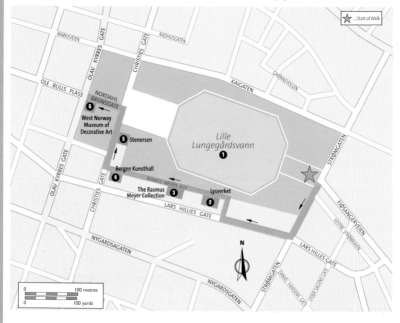

Bergen Art Museum (Kunstmuseum)
Tel: (47) 55 56 80 00.
www.bergenartmuseum.no. Open: mid-May–
mid-Sept daily 11am–5pm; mid-Sept–mid-
May Tue–Sun 11am–5pm. Admission charge.
Bergen Kunsthall
Tel: (47) 55 55 93 10. www.kunsthall.no.
Open: Tue–Sun noon–5pm. Admission charge.
West Norway Museum of Decorative Art
Nordahl Brunsgate 9. Tel: (47) 55 33 66 33.
www.vk.museum.no. Open: mid-May–mid-
Sept daily 11am–5pm; mid-Sept–mid-May
Tue–Sun noon–4pm. Admission charge.

world go by or for a picnic lunch in
fine weather.

2 Lysverket

A relative newcomer to the art gallery
district, this collection of Norwegian
and international art from the 15th
century to the present day opened in
2003. Among the greats on display here
are works by Joan Miró, Picasso and
Paul Klee. Also of note are the 14th-
century Russian and Greek icons and
17th-century Dutch paintings.
From Rasmus Meyers allé 9, pass on to
Rasmus Meyers allé 7.

3 The Rasmus Meyer Collection

Norway's greatest artist Edvard Munch
(*see pp19–20*) is well represented here,
with works such as *Melancholy* and
Jealousy, as are other native masters
including J C Dahl and Harriet Backer.
Other highlights include furniture and
furnishings from local homes from the
18th century and the painted walls and
ceiling of the Blumenthal Room.
Make your way to Rasmus Meyers allé 5.

4 Bergen Kunsthall

This is Bergen's main centre for the
display of contemporary art, with an
ever-changing series of exhibitions and
installations by contemporary artists
from around the world.
Head for Rasmus Meyers allé 3.

5 Stenersen

Formerly home to the modern art
collection that is now seen in Lysverket,
the Stenersen now hosts a continuous
circle of temporary exhibitions. To find
out what the current exhibitions are
during your stay, visit the tourist office
on Vågasllmenningen.
Turn right up Christies Gate and take the
first left into Nordahl Brunsgate.

6 West Norway Museum of Decorative Art

Norwegian silverware, ceramics, textiles
and the world's oldest-surviving violin
(1562) are among the exhibits in this
eclectic collection. The museum also
houses the largest gathering of
Buddhist sculptures in Northern
Europe and other Oriental figurines.

Old warehouses on the waterfront, Bergen

Bergen Akvariet (Bergen Aquarium)

Perched at the end of the Nordnes peninsula, Bergen's aquarium is one of the city's most popular attractions. Visitors can marvel at tanks full of Nordic marine life, but the main attractions are the seals and penguins. *Nordnesbakken 4.*
Tel: (47) 55 55 71 71. www.akvariet.com. Open: daily May–Aug 9am–7pm; Sept–Apr 10am–6pm. Penguin feeding time, performances of trained seal antics: daily noon, 3pm & 6pm. Admission charge.

Bergen Museum

Two different sites explore two different aspects of local history, cultural and natural. The cultural section includes remnants from the Viking era, folk art, church art, Norwegian myths and legends, and an area devoted to Henrik Ibsen. The natural history collection focuses on the various stages of evolution, geology, fossil life, whales and Norwegian bird life, among other things. *Harald Hårfagresgate 1.*
Tel: (47) 55 58 93 60.
www.bergenmuseum.uib.no. Open: June–Aug Tue–Fri 10am–4pm, Sat & Sun 11am–4pm; Sept–May Tue–Fri 10am–3pm, Sat & Sun 11am–4pm. Admission charge.

Bergens Sjøfartsmuseum (Bergen Maritime Museum)

The history of seafaring and shipbuilding in the region, from the

THE BUEKORPS

Unique to Bergen, the Buekorps (Archery Brigade) are an official boys' brigade who march through the city in spring in their uniforms, banging drums and waving flags. They take their origins from the Citizens' Guards that existed in every Norwegian city until the late 19th century. Bergen boys organised their own troops in imitation of their elders. Word spread, and soon many Norwegian towns had these defence guards. But it is only in Bergen that the tradition has continued. The theory is that the boys, aged between nine and fifteen, organise and manage themselves without adult intervention or preconceived ideas of race or class. There are now 12 corps in Bergen, whose marches in spring are considered an intrinsic part of the local landscape. The boys also involve themselves in sport, excursions and cultural activities, much the same as cubs and scouts in other countries.

Viking period to the present day, is presented in this museum. The collection includes archaeological finds and exhibits demonstrating what life was like on board over the centuries. *Håkon Sheteligs plass 15.*
Tel: (47) 55 54 96 00. www.bsj.uib.no. Open: June–Aug daily 11am–3pm; Sept–May Sun–Fri 11am–2pm. Admission charge.

Buekorps Museum

Devoted to the traditions and history of the Buekorps boys' brigade, which has now taken on the force of a social phenomenon, the museum details every aspect of the groups, from their costumes to their crossbows. It also helps promote the current corps.

Murhvelvingen. Tel: (47) 55 90 45 31. www.buekorps.museum.no. Open: Sat 11am–2pm, Sun noon–3pm. Closed: mid-July–mid-Aug. Admission charge.

Fisketorget (Fish Market)

One of the most distinctive images of the city after the Bryggen waterfront, Bergen's fish market is probably Norway's most famous market. Every day, a vast array of stalls, set up beneath brightly coloured canopies by hard-working fishmongers dressed in waterproofs and wellies, sells their catch on the harbour front. And what a catch it is. Apart from piles of prawns, cockles, crabs, oysters and lobster, there are catfish, monkfish and great slabs of whale meat. A bowl of freshly boiled shrimps, or a freshly made prawn or smoked salmon roll is not only delicious but is also a great budget lunch alternative to Norway's pricey restaurants. Adjacent to the fish market are souvenir stalls selling Norwegian handicrafts.

Torget. www.torgetibergen.no. Open: June–Aug daily 7am–7pm; Sept–May Mon–Sat 7am–4pm.

Fløibanen Funicular

The seven-minute funicular ride to the summit of Mount Fløien is a wonderful way to gain a panoramic perspective of the city as well as to embark on a number of marked trails

Fish stalls at the fish market in Bergen

A street in Bergen's Old Town

Kong Oscarsgate 59. Tel: (47) 48 16 26 78. www.lepra.no. Open: mid-May–Aug daily 11am–3pm. Admission charge.

Norges Fiskerimuseum (Norwegian Fisheries Museum)

The fishing industry has always been vital to the Norwegian economy, and this small museum dedicates itself to explaining all aspects of the business. Exhibits span the range from local marine life in the North Sea waters to boats and equipment and their development through the ages, as well as the more controversial aspects of whaling and sealing. Combine a visit to the museum with a trip to the fish market on the other side of the harbour, and you'll know all there is to know about how the catch ended up on the table.
Bontelabo 2. Tel: (47) 55 32 12 49. Open: June–Aug Mon–Fri 10am–6pm, Sat & Sun noon–4pm; Sept–May Mon–Fri 11am–4pm, Sun noon–4pm. Admission charge.

Ulriksbanen

The highest of Bergen's mountain backdrops is Mount Ulriken, and those with a strong stomach can take a cable car to its summit for breathtaking views of fjords and the island coastline. The cable car runs year round, but is subject to weather conditions, particularly in the winter.
Tel: (47) 55 20 20 20. www.ulriken.no. Operates daily June–Aug 9am–9pm; May & Sept 9am–5pm; Oct & Apr 10am–5pm. Admission charge.

in the mountains. The restaurant on the summit offers a very scenic lunch or dinner.
Vetrlidsalmenning 21. Tel: (47) 55 33 68 00. www.floibanen.no. Operates Mon–Fri 7.30am–11pm, Sat 8am–11pm, Sun 9am–11pm. Admission charge.

Lepramuseet (Leprosy Museum)

Leprosy is also known as Hansen's disease, after the Bergen-born doctor Armauer Hansen who pioneered research into the condition and its cure. Considerable work was done to help patients with the disease in the 18th-century St Jørgens Hospital. The wards have now been converted into a museum, which explores the lives of the courageous doctors and their charges.

AROUND BERGEN
Damsgård Manor
A beautiful 18th-century Baroque-style manor house, 3km (2 miles) outside Bergen, Damsgård Manor has extensive gardens and interiors preserved to look like they would have in the 1770s. *Alléen 39, Laksevåg. Tel: (47) 55 94 08 70. www.vk.museum.no. Open: mid-May–Aug daily 11am–4pm. Admission charge.*

Fantoft Stavkirke (Fantoft Stave Church)
Moved to Fantoft, 5km (3 miles) away from Bergen, from the fjord town of Fortun in the 19th century, the 12th-century stave church tragically burned down in 1992 in an arson attack. But it was promptly and lovingly rebuilt to its original design. *Paradis. Tel: (47) 55 28 07 10. Open: mid-May–mid-Sept daily 10.30am–2pm & 2.30–6pm. Admission charge.*

Lysøen Island
Lysøen means 'island of light', and the villa on this tiny island around 30km (19 miles) south of Bergen was the summer residence of Norway's legendary violinist Ole Bull (*see box, p58*). Its façade is a fanciful design combining traditional wooden clapboard architecture with ornate carvings and minarets reminiscent

The Fløibanen funicular ride provides a great view of Bergen

of the Orient, and earning from Bull the nickname 'Little Alhambra'. Inside are various pieces relating to Bull and his work, while the extensive grounds include marked trails.
Tel: (47) 56 30 90 77.
www.lysoen.no.
Open: mid-May–Aug Mon–Sat noon–4pm, Sun 11am–5pm; Sept Sun noon–4pm.
Admission charge.

Norsk Trikotasjemuseum (Norwegian Knitting Museum)

Norwegian knitwear is one of its most recognisable and popular crafts, so it is surprising that this museum, just north of the city, is the only one of its kind in the country. Set in a former knitwear factory, it clearly explains the whole process of producing the brightly coloured sweaters, from spinning the wool to the end result. Naturally there's also a shop so you can stock up on traditional woollies before you leave.
Salhus. Tel: (47) 55 25 10 80.
www.museumsnett.no/salhus.
Open: June–Aug Tue–Fri 11am–4pm, Sun 11am–6pm; Sept–May Tue–Fri 11am–3pm, Sun noon–4pm.

Old Bergen Museum

Bergen's Old Town (Gamle Bergen) buildings have been moved to Sandviken and gathered together under the umbrella of the Old Bergen Museum. This open-air area preserves around 40 wooden buildings, and in many cases, their original function,

OLE BULL

Norway's greatest violin virtuoso, Ole Bull (1810–80), specialised in performing Norwegian folk music to international audiences. Known as both a political idealist and an eccentric bon viveur who knew most of contemporary Europe's musicians and writers, he made his villa on Lysøen a regular meeting place for 19th-century society. A child prodigy, Bull joined his native Bergen's Philharmonic Orchestra at the age of eight, but soon became known beyond his country's borders and travelled the world to give concerts, particularly in the United States. But his love for Norway never left him. He founded the Norwegian Theatre in Bergen, and attempted to create a centre for Norwegian Folk Music, but could never secure enough funding for the latter project. Bull was also a great influence on Grieg, who was encouraged to study music by the violinist.

such as a bakery, a shop and a sailor's home. The area is free to be explored on foot at any time of the year, but to get the most out of the history of this beautiful region and to enter any of the buildings, it is necessary to take a guided tour, which are held on the hour.
Nyhavnsveien 4.
Tel: (47) 55 39 43 00.
www.gamlebergen.no.
Open: May–Aug daily 9.30am–6.30pm.
Admission charge (for tours).

Siljustøl

Located 12km (7 miles) away from Bergen, this was the residence of Harald Sæverud (1897–1992), the most respected Norwegian composer of the

20th century. Sæverud himself designed the house, which is based on traditional Norwegian buildings and natural materials. It is now a museum commemorating his life and work, in particular the rousing protest music composed during Norway's occupation by the Nazis during World War II.

Rådal. Tel: (47) 55 92 29 92. www.siljustol.no. Open: mid-June–mid-Sept Sun noon–4pm. Admission charge.

Troldhaugen

Norway's greatest composer Edvard Grieg (*see p20*) lived in this white clapboard house just outside Bergen for more than 20 years with his wife Nina, and composed many of his most famous works here. He and his wife are buried in the grounds. Today, the house has been turned into a museum to honour the composer's life, and the interior has been preserved to look as it would have done in 1907, the year that Grieg died. Sections of music manuscripts and other personal belongings can also be seen in the garden hut where Grieg worked. The Troldsalen concert hall stages classical music performances during the summer.

Hop. Tel: (47) 55 92 29 92. www.troldhaugen.com. Open: May–Sept daily 9am–6pm; Oct–Nov & mid-Jan–Apr Mon–Fri 10am–2pm, Sat & Sun noon–4pm. Admission charge.

The exterior of the Troldsalen concert hall in Troldhaugen

Southern Norway

With its central position between the two main cities, Oslo and Bergen, its abundance of beaches in the Sørlandet region and its balmy climate in summer, southern Norway receives more visitors than any other region of the country, except perhaps the fjords. Inland, hills and valleys make for excellent walking and cycling terrain, and the beautiful Telemark district is a haven for boaters who ply its canal leisurely. Kristiansand and Stavanger are two cities that deserve exploration, while those interested in history will revel in the area's abundance of Viking sites and remnants of Swedish invasions.

KRISTIANSAND

The main city on Norway's south coast is often referred to as the 'Summer City' because of its beaches and resort-town ambience, complete with harbourside restaurants and cafés. The fact that it is an industrial and transportation hub does not take away from its charm in any way.

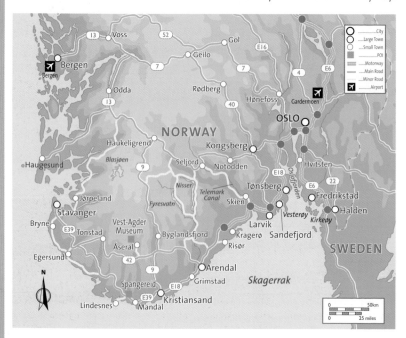

Climb the Domkirke's tower for wonderful views of Kristiansand and the surrounding area

Walk: Central Kristiansand

A compact area, made even easier to navigate by its grid-like street design, Central Kristiansand contains most of the city's sights and is best explored by a leisurely stroll.

Allow about 4–5 hours for the walk to take in all the sights, including lunch on the waterfront, but a full day if taking a ferry cruise to one of the islands.

Start at Kirkegata.

1 Domkirke

Norway's largest church, Kristiansand's cathedral was completed in 1884. The most popular time to visit the Gothic-style cathedral is summer, when various music concerts are held here, but you can climb to the top of the tower at any time of the year.

Continue along Kirkegata and turn left into Skippergata.

2 Sørlandets Kunstmuseum (Sørlandet Art Museum)

Norwegian art from 1800 to the present is exhibited here. A ground-floor hall presents film screenings, concerts and art exhibitions.

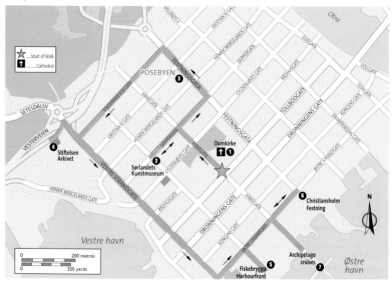

On leaving the museum, turn right and continue along Skippergata until you reach Festningsgata. Turn left to reach the streets that make up the Posebyen district.

3 Posebyen

Kristiansand's old town district is a collection of low-level wooden buildings from the 17th to the 19th centuries. Rather deserted, it preserves a feel of days gone by. Among the highlights is the house at *Elvegata 39*, built in 1698. Another building from the same era (1695) is at *Kronprinsens gate 45*, once a textile and timber warehouse and post office. The Sløyden house at *Gyldenløvesgata 70* was used for religious services until it became a boys' school in the late 19th century.

If visiting on a Saturday in summer, don't miss the street market in Holbergs

gate (11am–4pm). Follow Tordenskjolds gate westwards to Vesterveien.

4 Stiftelsen Arkivet (Archive Centre)

This building housed the Nazi German headquarters during World War II. Many historical details from that era are preserved, but now it is a humanitarian centre against conflict.

Head south down Vestre Strandgate towards the harbour.

5 Fiskebrygga Harbourfront

Once a run-down area, Kristiansand's waterfront now makes for a pleasant stroll. There are restaurants here, with open-air terraces offering live entertainment in summer.

Follow the waterfront eastwards to Festningsgata.

6 Christiansholm Festning (Christiansholm Fortress)

Kristiansand's fortress was built in 1672 to protect the harbour from Swedish invasion and pirates.

Retrace your steps to the harbourfront.

7 Archipelago cruises

If the weather is nice, board a boat and sail around the archipelago of *skerries* (little islands) just off the city's mainland. Activities and sights in islands such as Bragdøy include bathing areas, walks and remnants of old wooden boats. Various companies along the harbour offer cruises throughout the summer.

Domkirke
Kirkegata. Tel: (47) 38 10 77 05. Open: June–Aug Mon–Fri 10am–4pm, Sat 10am–2pm. Tower open: July–mid-Aug 11am & 2pm. Free admission.

Sørlandets Kunstmuseum
Skippergata 24B. Tel: (47) 38 07 49 00. www.skmu.no. Open: Tue–Sun noon–4pm. Closed: Mon. Admission charge.

Stiftelsen Arkivet
Vesterveien 4. Tel: (47) 38 10 74 00. www.stiftelsen-arkivet.no. Open: May–Aug 8.30am–3pm; Sept–Apr 8.30am–3.30pm. Admission charge.

Christiansholm Festning
Festningsgata. Tel: (47) 38 07 51 50. Open: mid-May–mid-Sept, 9am–9pm. Free admission.

Archipelago cruises
www.sorlandet.com

An unusual loft next to the fish market

Around Central Kristiansand
Agder-Naturmuseum & Botaniske Hage (Nature Museum & Botanical Gardens)

This well-planned museum uncovers the region's natural history from the last Ice Age to the present day, examining local geology and wildlife. Among the exhibits are minerals found locally. Outside, a botanical garden includes a rose garden that has been flourishing here since the mid-19th century, and, incongruously this far north, a cactus garden, as well as many other plants.
Gimleveien 23. Tel: (47) 38 09 23 88. Open: mid-Aug–mid-June Tue–Fri 10am–3pm, Sun noon–4pm. Admission charge.

Dyreparken (Kristiansand Zoo & Amusement Park)

Located 11km (7 miles) outside Kristiansand centre, Norway's most popular theme park and children's attraction (*see p160*) re-creates various landscapes from around the world. The Scandinavian 'wilderness' features animals indigenous to the Nordic landscape, including reindeer, elk and wolves. The African plains are re-created in a section called My Africa, where a raised boardwalk offers views of animals such as giraffes and zebras. There's also a rainforest area, with monkeys swinging from tree to tree, while other habitats provide homes to kangaroos, llamas and sea lions. Like most zoos today, Dyreparken is heavily involved in the protection of endangered species and breeding programmes. One section that will mean little to non-Norwegian children is Cardamom Town, based on the work of the children's book author, Thorbjørn Egner, but there's also an authentic pirate ship and a water park that will delight kids of any nationality.
Kardemomme By. Tel: (47) 38 04 97 00. www.dyreparken.com. Open: daily June–Aug 10am–5pm; Sept–May 10am–3pm. Admission charge.

Kanonmuseet (Kristiansand Cannon Museum)

Kristiansand was an important defence region during World War II, and this museum exhibits many items from that

era, as well as the world's largest on land cannon, weighing 337 tonnes.
Møvik. Tel: (47) 38 08 50 90. Open: mid-Aug–Sept Mon–Wed 11am–3pm, Thur–Sun 11am–5pm; Oct Sun 11am–5pm. During July, the cannon is fired every Wed between 4pm & 5pm. Admission charge.

Ravenedalen Nature Park
Just to the northwest of the town centre is this wonderfully peaceful park with a wide range of trees and plants, as well as lakes dotted with swans. In summer, the park is a venue for concerts and open-air theatre productions. Other attractions include a range of hiking trails and, in winter, skiing opportunities.

Vest-Agder Fylkesmuseum (West Agder Folk Museum)
This open-air museum re-creates a period street from Kristiansand (Bygaden) and a complex of farm buildings. There are also areas devoted to maritime history, vintage cars, children's toys, regional costumes and an exhibit about the resistance movement in the area during World War II.
Kongsgård. Tel: (47) 38 09 02 28. www.museumsnett.no/vafymuseum. Open: mid-June–mid-Aug Tue–Fri

The harbour at Kristiansand

*10am–6pm & Sat–Mon noon–6pm;
mid-Aug–mid-June Sun noon–5pm.
Admission charge.*

ØSTFOLD & VESTFOLD

Those without the time to cross the
country to the main fjord region in the
west could do worse than enjoy the
delights of the Oslofjord, flowing out
from the capital. Historic towns such as
Frederikstad and Tønsberg are
highlights of this region, while the
offshore islands are perfect idylls for
bathing and cycling.

Fredrikstad

Named in honour of King Fredrik II,
the main draw of Fredrikstad is its
well-preserved 17th-century Old
Town (Gamlebyen). Because of its
intermediary role as a trading centre
between European nations, the town
was fortified in 1663, to protect it
against a possible Swedish invasion in
particular. The resulting moats and
walls, which were once protected by 200
cannons, can still be seen. It was a futile
measure – the Swedes arrived 15 years
later and took over the town and the
fortress (Kongsten Festning), which can
still be visited just outside the town.

Fredrikstad Museum

Set within original period buildings,
this museum explores the history of
the town, particularly its complicated
military past. Another site of the
museum is the island of Isegran across
the Glomma River, where the ruins of

A bust of Roald Amundsen at the Centre

a 13th-century fortress can be seen.
*Tøihusgaten 41. Tel: (47) 69 95 85 00.
www.fredrikstad.kommune.no/museet.
Open: May–Sept Mon–Fri 11am–5pm,
Sat & Sun noon–5pm. Closed: Oct–Apr.
Admission charge.*

Roald Amundsen Centre

Approximately 7km (4 miles) outside
Fredrikstad is the birthplace of the great
Norwegian explorer Roald Amundsen
(*see pp46–7*). His home now lovingly
documents his brave expeditions to the
North and South Poles.
*Framveien 9, Hvidsten. Tel: (47) 69 34
83 26. Open: Mon–Thur 10am–8pm.
Admission charge.*

Halden

Strategically located near the southern borders of Norway and Sweden, Halden was the frequent focus of fierce invasions during the 17th and 18th centuries. The need, therefore, arose for a powerful fortress as a protective measure.

Fredriksten Festning (Fredriksten Fortress)

Despite its name, this is not to be confused with the fortress in Fredrikstad. Commissioned by King Fredrick III in 1660 in an attempt to fend off the threatening Swedes across the border, this star-shaped complex of alleyways and gates is still, in part, used by the Norwegian army. However, areas such as storehouses and powderhouses have now been given over to museums and tourist attractions. The War Museum details not only the battles with Sweden in the distant past, but also the more recent terror of Nazi occupation during World War II. The Byen Brenner museum explores the locals' habit of setting fire to their town rather than giving in to Swedish invasions; an act that is noted in the Norwegian national anthem. Other evocative features include re-creations of an old-style bakery, brewery and pharmacy.
Pede Colbjørnsens Gate.
Tel: (47) 69 18 31 49.
Open: mid-May–Aug daily 10am–5pm;
Sept Sun noon–3pm.
Admission charge.

Hvaler

This series of islands just offshore from Oslofjord is a summer haven for Norwegians, particularly Oslo residents escaping city life. They are particularly popular with cyclists for their easy-going air and lack of heavy traffic. There are more than 500 islands, the most visited being Vesterøy, Akerøy with its 17th-century fortress, Asmaløy and Kirkeøy with its charming medieval church.

Larvik

Most people pass through Larvik either en route to or arriving from Denmark by the ferry service that docks here, or to head off for the holiday resort area of the Brunlanes Peninsula, but it is an interesting enough town in its own right.
The main centre of tourist activity is the **Larvik Museum**, which is divided into three sections: a maritime museum is home to model ships and has a section devoted to native-born Thor Heyerdahl (*see p47*); the Fritzøe Museum focuses on the region's iron industry; and a 17th-century manor house is preserved with antiques at Herregården.
Larvik Museum: Nedre Fritzøegate 2.
Tel: (47) 33 17 12 90. Open: mid-
June–mid-Aug daily 10am–5pm.
Admission charge.

Sandefjord

The main attraction of Sandefjord, 130km (81 miles) south of Oslo, is as a summer recreation area, either for sunbathing and picnicking on its beaches, or hiring out boats. Like its neighbour Tønsberg, there are plenty of museums in town to document Sandefjord's past as a wealthy and important centre of the whaling industry, but it is the laid-back atmosphere, fishermen on the harbour and general sense of ease and relaxation that bring visitors here, year after year.

Tønsberg

Historians claim that Tønsberg is Norway's oldest town, believed to have been settled by the Vikings in around AD 871 and mentioned in the sagas. While its current scenery doesn't date back anywhere near that far, there is still a pleasant area of preserved wooden houses within its historic district, Nordbyen. Other attractions include a 12th-century church and the ruins of a hilltop fortress, offering great views of the town. Tønsberg is also the home of Jarlsberg, Norway's 'national' cheese.

Vestfold Fylkesmuseum (Vestfold Folk Museum)

This museum stands as testament to the town's Viking past and to its more recent (19th-century) contribution to the country's whaling industry: the exploding harpoon, for instance, was invented here. There is a detailed explanation about the project to raise the Viking ship *Oseberg* that

THE WHITE TOWNS

The typical traditional Norwegian house is a wooden clapboard home, painted a dark russet red. In southern Norway, however, there are several towns that are known as the 'white towns' for their distinctive whitewashed façades. During the 19th century, when the area began to trade with the Netherlands and Britain, the Norwegians were inspired by Dutch and British architecture to paint their houses white, despite the fact that white paint was expensive at the time. They thus not only brightened the landscape but also became symbols of prestige, and even decadence. The whitewashed look of towns such as Arendal, Risør and Grimstad has been preserved, and today the old buildings house chic craft shops and cafés.

was found near here and is now displayed in Olso's Vikingskiphuset (*see p40*), while a skeleton of a captured blue whale is an impressive sight. A farm area exhibits farm buildings over the centuries.
Frarmannsveien 30.
Tel: (47) 33 31 29 19. www.vfm.no.
Open: Mon–Sat 11am–4pm, Sun noon–4pm.
Admission charge.

THE SOUTH COAST

With its proximity to the nation's capital, the south coast swells with urbanites in summer escaping from the city streets. Most take boating and beach holidays along the waterfront, staying at traditional resort towns such as Arendal and Risør, with their classic 19th-century architecture.

Arendal

One of the oldest towns in Sørlandet, Arendal has a well-preserved town centre, known as Tyholmen, with wooden buildings that date back to the 17th century. Its picturesque setting draws artists and artisans, who sell their wares in the area. The town hall is reputedly Norway's tallest building constructed entirely in timber. Just offshore from Arendal, the island of Merdø is a popular bathing spot. The island's museum consists of an 18th-century sea captain's home with furniture and fittings from that time.

Aust-Agder Museum

Due to its coastal location, Arendal has always been a seafaring town, and this fascinating museum displays artefacts that intrepid sailors brought home with

The old town of Arendal on the Skagerrak

them after their journeys around the world. It is an intriguing insight into the distances travelled and the items considered relevant to bring home as souvenirs from far-off lands. There is also an exhibition about life in the town during World War II, and a random collection of historic toys, carriages and furniture.

Parkveien 16. Tel: (47) 37 07 35 00. www.aaks.no. Open: mid-June–mid-Aug Mon–Fri 9am–5pm, Sun noon–5pm; mid-Aug–mid-June Mon–Fri 9am–3pm, Sun noon–3pm. Admission charge.

Kløckers Hus (Kløckers House)

Built in 1826, this former private home has been turned into a museum to illustrate the life of the wealthy between 1600 and 1800. All the rooms, including a dining room, an office and a wash-house, are furnished with period details.

Nedre Tyholmsvei 14. Tel: (47) 37 02 59 25. www.arendal.com. Open: Sept–July Tue–Fri 9am–3pm, Sat & Sun 10am–2pm. Admission charge.

Grimstad

Locals claim that there are more hours of sunshine in Grimstad than anywhere else in the country, which, whether true or not, unsurprisingly makes this laid-back, whitewashed town a popular holiday destination. It wasn't always this peaceful, however; during the late 19th century, the town was the busiest ship- and boat-building area in Norway.

50km (31 miles) from Kristiansand on Highway E18.

Grimstad Bymuseum-Ibsenhuset (Grimstad Town Museum & Ibsen House)

Another nod to this Norwegian great can be found at this old pharmacy and house where Ibsen lived and worked before making playwrighting his full-time profession. Many of his personal belongings are on display here.
Henrik Ibsen Gate 14.
Tel: (47) 37 04 04 90. www.ibsen.net.
Open: May–Aug Mon–Sat 11am–5pm,
Sun noon–5pm. Admission charge.

Kragerø

The pretty narrow lanes and whitewashed wooden houses of this waterfront town have made it a favoured holiday spot in summer. There is a statue of Edvard Munch in the town in honour of the summers he spent here painting the coastal landscape that he so admired.
150km (93 miles) from Kristiansand on Highway E18.

Lindesnes Fyr (Lindesnes Lighthouse)

The most southerly point of Norway is the site of the country's first lighthouse, built in 1656, although the current building dates from 1916. Today, it houses a museum documenting the history of lighthouses along the Norwegian coast, as well as the lives of the lighthouse keepers.
Stiftelsen Lindesnes Fyrmuseum.
Tel: (47) 97 54 08 15.

www.lindesnesfyr.no. Open: Oct–Mar Sat & Sun 11am–5pm; Apr–June & mid-Aug–Sept daily 11am–5pm; July–mid-Aug daily 9am–9pm. Admission charge.

Mandal

This picturesque town east of Lindesnes has whitewashed timber buildings set against a backdrop of deep-green pine forests. Its claim to fame is that it has one of the most popular beaches in the country, Sjøsanden.

Vigeland House Museum

The childhood home of artist Gustav Vigeland, who created Oslo's sculpture park (*see p42*), exhibits various pieces of his work.
Tel: (47) 38 27 83 00.
Open: mid-June–mid-Aug Tue–Sun noon–4pm. Admission charge.

The Lindesnes Lighthouse, the first to be built in Norway

Risør

Lined with boats bobbing on the water and whitewashed wooden buildings, Risør's scenic harbour front has made it a perennially popular holiday spot for both Norwegians and visitors, many of whom are artists who come here each summer to work and sell their paintings. An added attraction is the numerous ferries to the offshore islands, which make for enjoyable day-trips.

120km (75 miles) from Kristiansand on Highway E18.

Risør Saltvannsakvariet (Risør Aquarium)

The saltwater aquarium here is a great way to become acquainted with the fish and crustaceans that inhabit the coastal waters of the region. The tanks are divided into different sections, such as the tidal zone and the deep-sea zone. Also included are a detailed exhibition on the life of a lobster and lobster farming, and a display of stuffed specimens of bird species that live along the coast.

Tel: (47) 37 15 32 82.
www.risorakvarium.no.
Open: mid-June–mid-Aug daily 11am–6pm; mid-Aug–mid-June Sat & Sun noon–4pm. Admission charge.

Spangereid Vikingland

An important base for Vikings during their heyday, Spangereid has now been turned into a historical centre focusing on the lives and times of these great warriors. There are numerous marked trails to Viking burial mounds, but perhaps the most exciting feature is the chance to go on a voyage on a Viking ship.

72km (45 miles) from Kristiansand.
Tel: (47) 38 27 76 61.
www.vikinglandspangereid.no.
Open: mid-June–Aug daily 11am–5pm. Admission charge.

STAVANGER & THE SOUTHERN FJORDS

The fourth-largest city in Norway, Stavanger is also its most cosmopolitan. This is mainly because, as the centre of the country's oil industry, it brings in oil workers from all over the world. Its Old Town and harbour are worth a stroll, but most tourists use the city as a setting-off point to head inland and explore the southern fjords such as Lysefjord and Boknafjorden.

Haugesund

Traditionally a herring-fishing and copper-mining town, Haugesund's main tourist draw is the Haraldshaugen Viking burial site of King Harald Hårfagre. Nearby is another mound with a Christian cross dating from the 11th century, which is an interesting landmark in the country's transition from pagan beliefs to Christianity. A rather incongruous monument can be found on the waterfront honouring the film star Marilyn Monroe: her father is said to have hailed from Haugesund.

80km (50 miles) from Stavanger.

Lysefjord

The nearest fjord to Stavanger, the 'light fjord' derives its name from the radiant light that seems to shine here any day of the year. Those with a head for heights can take the trail to the summit of the Preikestolen rock, which offers breathtaking views. At the head of the fjord is Lysebotn, which has one of Norway's most famous sets of switchback mountain roads.

Stavanger

Most visitors to the area find themselves in Stavanger at some point in their trip, whether as a landing point by air or boat, or as a port of call while travelling from the south coast to the fjords or vice versa. While it certainly lacks the appeal of nearby Bergen, the city deserves at least a day's exploration. Its most evocative part is Gamle Stavanger (Old Town),

Stavanger city

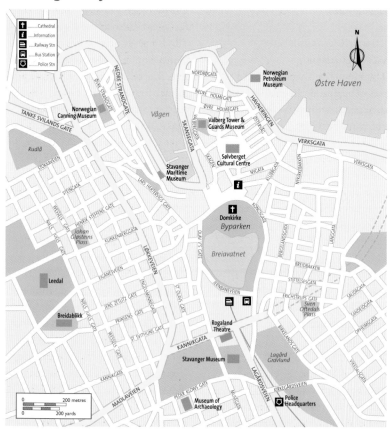

where 18th-century buildings have been lovingly preserved and restored, and are now prime locations for residents despite their lower-class beginnings. The narrow lanes of whitewashed timber homes, enhanced by 19th-century lanterns, offer an experience far more stirring than many of the country's re-created open-air museums.

In 2008 Stavanger is the European City of Culture, an honour that the city hopes will highlight its cultural activities then and in the years to come.

Arkeologisk Museum
(Museum of Archaeology)

Everything you could possibly need to know about the region's prehistoric past is displayed here in an entertaining yet educational manner. There are dioramas of life in prehistoric times, as well as plenty of exhibits designed for children to engage them in what can be rather dry subject matter.
Peder Klows gate 30A.
Tel: (47) 51 84 60 04.
www.ark.museum.no.
Open: June–Aug Tue–Sun 11am–5pm; Sept–May Tue 11am–8pm, Wed–Sat 11am–3pm, Sun 11am–4pm. Admission charge.

Domkirke

A blend of Romanesque, Gothic and Baroque architecture, this 12th-century cathedral was restored to its original style in the early 20th century. The Baroque influence is most noticeable in the pulpit, which is carved with scenes from the Old Testament. It is believed that the church's collection of relics includes the arm of St Swithun, the patron saint of the cathedral.
Håkon VII's gate 2. Tel: (47) 51 89 57 83.
Open: Mon–Tue 11am–2pm, Wed–Sat 10am–3pm. Free admission.

Norsk Oljemuseum
(Norwegian Petroleum Museum)

It may seem strange to have a museum devoted exclusively to oil, but this is a measure of the importance of the industry to Norway. The discovery of oil deposits off the Norwegian coast in 1969 changed the country dramatically, and here one can find out why. The design of the museum reflects the industrial nature of its subject, with its heavy use of steel and tin, while a re-created oil rig explains the science behind drilling for oil as well as life on the platform for the oilmen who spend many months each year on these isolated North Sea posts.
Kjeringholmen. Tel: (47) 51 93 93 00.
www.norskolje.museum.no.
Open: June–Aug daily 10am–7pm; Sept–May Mon–Sat 10am–4pm, Sun 10am–6pm. Admission charge.

Stavanger Museum

Under the umbrella of one name, the Stavanger Museum actually consists of five different sites, which explore five very different aspects of the city and its surroundings. All five have the same telephone number and follow the same opening times, apart from the fact that the Leedal and Breidablikk houses and the Maritime Museum close in winter.

Located opposite one another, **Leedal** and **Breidablikk** were originally merchants' houses, the former dating from 1799 and the latter from 1881. Both are preserved to look as they would have in the days when they were inhabited. Leedal becomes the official royal residence when the region is visited by the monarchy.

The **Norsk Hermitkkmuseum (Norwegian Canning Museum)** is the most unusual and probably the most interesting of the five museums. Until the 1960s, Stavanger was central to the Norwegian fish canning industry, and this old converted canning factory shows every aspect of the laborious process of filling tins with sardines and herrings. Nothing is left to the imagination and nothing is romanticised; this was a tough life and no visitor will leave the museum with any other impression. The only

A house covered in winter snow in Telemark

sense of nostalgia is generated by the display of old tins and their artistic images of friendly fisherfolk. Try to visit on the first Sunday of the month when the smoking ovens are cranked up and visitors can taste freshly smoked brisling.

As its name would suggest, the main **Stavanger Museum** details the history of Stavanger, from the Viking era to the present day.

Set in an 18th-century warehouse, the atmospheric **Stavanger Sjøfartsmuseum (Maritime Museum)** focuses on all aspects of the city's life on the west coast. Models of ships, fishermen's homes, seafaring equipment and maps, as well as information about the herring and oil industry, are all represented here.
Tel: (47) 51 84 27 00.
www.stavanger.museum.no.
Open: mid-June–mid-Aug daily 11am–4pm. Admission charge.
Leedal & Breidablikk: Eiganesveien 40A & 45. Closed: Dec–Jan.
Norsk Hermitkkmuseum: Øvre Strandgate 88A.
Stavanger Museum: Muségata 16.
Stavanger Sjøfartsmuseum: Nedre Strandgate 17–19. Closed: Dec.

TELEMARK & THE INLAND REGION

A striking setting of lakes and canals in summer and cross-country skiing opportunities in winter, the Telemark region is one of the best known in Norway for holidaymakers all year round, particularly for those who thrive on the great outdoors.

Åseral

In the wild, mountainous regions of Åseral is a wide range of trails and hiking opportunities, past babbling streams and panoramic views of the area. Some hikes are a short 3km (2-mile) stretch, while others require an overnight stay at designated tourist cabins. The main starting points are Ljosland, Eikerapen and Bortelid.
85km (53 miles) from Kristiansand.
Tel: (47) 38 27 83 00.
www.regionmandal.com

Byglandsfjorden

One of the most memorable experiences of the region is to sail the Byglandsfjorden aboard Norway's only remaining steamship fired by wood, the D/S *Bjoren*, built in 1866. The *Bjoren* was in regular use until the 1950s, when the advent of roads made it redundant. Now, it has found another, much-appreciated use as a vessel for tourists to sail across this 40km (25-mile) lake.
Evje. Tel: (47) 37 93 14 00.

Kongsberg

From the early 17th century until the late 1950s, Kongsberg was the scene of Norway's major silver rush, when mines were opened and consistently exploited after the discovery of 'white gold' beneath the ground. The main beneficiary was the king, hence the name Kongsberg, which translates as 'king's town'. Silversmithing is still a major trade in the country. The town's main tourist draw is a tour of the old mines, even though they have long since ceased to be operational.
78km (48 miles) from Oslo.

Kongsberg Domkirke

Built in a mix of Baroque and Rococo styles, the town's large church is, unsurprisingly, filled with numerous silver decorative pieces, hewn from the nearby mines.
Kirketorget. Tel: (47) 33 73 19 02.
Open: mid-May–Aug Mon–Fri
10am–4pm, Sat 10am–1pm & Sun
2–4pm; Sept–mid-May Tue–Thur
10am–noon. Admission charge.

Kongsberg Sølvgruver (Silver Mines)

Just outside the centre of town are the old silver mines that explain, in atmospheric detail, the history of the industry in the region, beginning from 1623. A specially designed train takes visitors through a man-made tunnel and deep into the mines, where mining equipment can be seen. Tourists also get a taste of the often hair-raising conditions under which the miners had to work. Warm clothing is advised whatever the time of year. For the more adventurous, there is also an abseiling tour deep into the Prince Fredrik mine, but this must be arranged in advance through the Norwegian Mining Museum.
Saggrenda. Tel: (47) 32 72 32 00.
Tours: 18 May–30 June & 15 Aug–31

Aug 11am, 1pm & 3pm. 1 July–14 Aug hourly from 11am (last departure 4pm). Sept Sat & Sun noon & 2pm. Oct Sun noon & 2pm. Will run outside of opening hours on request for additional fee. Admission charge.

Norsk Bergverksmuseum (Norwegian Mining Museum)

If you don't want to make the journey out of town, or are nervous about descending so deep below ground to see the actual mines, the central mining museum will explain all you need to know about this 'boom period' in Kongsberg's history. Complete with smelting furnaces and other mining paraphernalia, the museum also has a section devoted to the minting of coins (the Norwegian Mint is located in Kongsberg).

Smelteyhytta. Tel: (47) 32 72 32 00. Open: mid-May–Aug daily 10am–5pm; Sept–mid-May daily noon–4pm. Admission charge.

Heddal stave church, Notodden

Just outside the town of Notodden, located 110km (68 miles) from Oslo, is one of Norway's most visited stave churches (*see pp98–9*). The largest surviving stave church in the country, this dates from the mid-13th century, and was restored in the 1950s when Norway became aware of the architectural significance of these structures. Inside are beautiful *rosmaling (*rose paintings) typical of these churches, and an altarpiece, all

dating from the 17th century. Adjacent to the structure is a small museum describing the history of the church and stave constructions in general.
Heddalsveien 412, N-3676 Notodden. Tel: (47) 35 02 04 00. www.heddal-stavkirke.no. Open: mid-May–mid-June & mid-Aug–mid-Sept Mon–Fri 10am–5pm, Sun 1–5pm; mid-June–mid-Aug Mon–Fri 9am–7pm, Sun 1–7pm. Admission charge.

Seljord

Most visitors stop off in the small town of Seljord to visit the lake that the so-called monster Selma is supposed to inhabit (*see p101*). Within the town, the Sea Serpent Centre explains the theories behind this mythical beast and sightings of her over the centuries. This rural region is, in fact, steeped in legends, and is also renowned for being the setting of the folk tale *The Three Billy Goats Gruff*, one of the few Norwegian stories to have found international fame.
195km (121 miles) north of Kristiansand.

Setesdalsbanen

Originally set up to transfer nickel from the region's mines, this late 19th-century steam train runs for 78km (48 miles) along a narrow-gauge railway through the Setesdalen valley from Kristiansand to Byglandsfjord. A trip in the comfort of this historic locomotive is a wonderful way to take in the

region's gorgeous scenery of green pastureland, mountains and forests.
Grovane. Tel: (47) 38 15 64 82.
www.sorlandet.com

Skien

The home town of Norway's greatest playwright, Henrik Ibsen (*see p21*), naturally devotes most of its attractions to honouring its literary giant. But if you are travelling with children, don't miss the water park at Bø Sommarland, the country's largest such theme park (*see p160*).
127km (79 miles) southeast of Oslo.

Brekkeparken

Rooms within this 18th-century manor house have been redesigned to emulate Ibsen's apartment in Oslo, including his study. There are also other interesting items of folk art, an open-air museum that includes an authentic old shop and tearooms, and a large garden and a field of tulips.
Øvregate 41. Tel: (47) 35 54 45 00.
www.telemark.museum.no.
Open: mid-May–Aug, daily 10am–6pm.
Admission charge.

Nordre Venstøp

Just outside town is the original farmhouse where Ibsen grew up. Many of the rooms, including the servants' quarters and a brewery, have been preserved in the manner in which the family would have furnished them. The young Ibsen is said to have displayed his theatrical inclination by staging puppet shows on the porch. It is claimed that Ibsen had the house's dank attic in mind while establishing the garret setting in one of his most famous plays, *The Wild Duck.*
Ventstophogda 74. Tel: (47) 35 52 35 94.
Open: mid-May–Aug daily 10am–6pm & Sept Sun 10am–6pm.
Admission charge.

Telemark Canal

At the end of the 19th century, a 105km (65-mile) canal was carved through the mountains of central southern Norway to offer easier access between the eastern and western parts of the country. Today, it is one of the country's most popular holiday areas, offering idyllic landscapes of mountain streams and dense forests.

In summer, various companies offer cruises along the route, crossing 28 locks along the way. Boats and canoes can also be hired for independent travel. In winter, the area is a skiing mecca, which is not surprising as it is considered by most to be the home of modern skiing (*see pp78–9*).
www.telemarkskanalen.com

Lake Seljord, said to be home to the legendary monster Selma

Norway's national sport

If any country in the world can claim to have a 'national sport', it is Norway. From the time they can stand on their own two legs, all Norwegian children learn how to ski, and what to many of us would seem a luxury break is to Norwegians a regular winter afternoon's jaunt.

Skiing in Norway is not a modern phenomenon. In Tro in the Nordland region (*see pp116–17*), Stone Age paintings depicting a man on skis prove that very early on, wooden boards were used as an ideal way to traverse the snowy landscape. The sledge is likely to have preceded the ski, which became a vital means of transport in many regions, not only for hunting and trapping, but also to commute to other settlements.

By the 17th century, the Norwegian army had begun to use skis as a convenient and fast means of getting around, but it wasn't until the 19th century that skiing began to be seen as a competitive sport. The first documented race, including ski jumping, was held in Tromsø in 1843, and in 1877 a skiing school was established in Oslo. Around this time, the design of skis began to change: the Telemark ski, as it is still known,

Mountainous Norway provides ideal skiing conditions

Skiing is enjoyed by both locals and visitors

was shaped with a 'waist' allowing easier and swifter manoeuvrability. But it was perhaps the explorer Fridtjof Nansen (*see pp46–7*) who was responsible for triggering off the craze, when he published his account of skiing across Greenland in 1890. The book was a great success and raised a greater international interest in the sport. In 1892, ski jumping events began in Holmenkollen, outside Oslo (*see p42*), and it has held centre stage ever since.

The first skiing sensation was Sondre Norheim (1825–97), from the Morgedal Valley in the Telemark region. He made a splash at the first national skiing competition held in Oslo in 1868 with his immense skill and his use of a new technique, which came to be known as the Telemark Turn. Norheim used shorter skis and heel rather than toe bindings, which allowed for advanced aptitude on the slopes. The artistry and sheer enjoyment that he displayed inspired others to treat skiing as a recreational sport rather than a means of transport. Norheim thus came to be known as the 'father of modern skiing', and the Olympic torch has been lit in his home town thrice.

The modern-day ski industry, as we now know it, really began to catch on in the early 20th century, when Europe's high society would hit the slopes of Switzerland or France, mostly under the tutelage of Norwegian instructors. But a great deal of its popularity in Norway can be attributed to the winter Olympic Games in Oslo in 1952, when the local champion Stein Eriksen was crowned, and the rise of mass tourism that began in the ensuing decades. Remarkably, however, given their influence in the sport, Norwegian resorts remain relatively homogeneous and have not seen the vast influx of tourists that flock annually to the Alps or Pyrenees.

While downhill skiing and jumping are popular sports in Norway, cross-country skiing is also an important competitive sport and pastime, affording an opportunity for physical challenge and to experience the snowy wilderness.

The Norwegian fjords

A unique aspect of Norway's landscape and one of its biggest attractions for tourists is its fjords: long, deep and narrow inlets carved out by retreating glaciers during the last Ice Age. The southwestern region has the highest concentration of fjords. There can be few things more relaxing than a gentle sail through these majestic fissures filled with crystal-clear waters and surrounded by majestic ice-topped mountains and gushing waterfalls.

The Norwegian fjords are an exciting region for the active traveller too, offering white-water rafting, hiking, horse riding and cycling, as well as daring climbs on spectacular glaciers for those with a good head for heights.

HARDANGER

Known as the 'garden of Norway', the Hardanger region, around 150km (93 miles) east of Bergen, erupts with colour in spring when its cherry and apple trees burst into life after a long,

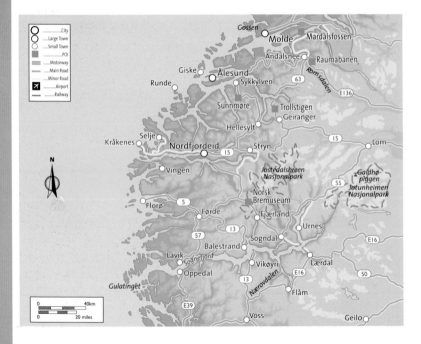

HARDANGER REGIONAL COSTUMES

Until World War II, most Norwegians dressed in traditional costumes daily, but now they are reserved for holidays. Every region of Norway has a distinctive folk costume (*bunad*), but it is the Hardanger dress that is the most familiar. The classic costume for women is an embroidered blouse worn under a red felt waistcoat (breastplate) and a black skirt, over which is worn a belt and an apron embroidered in the famed Hardanger style: white thread on white linen. The bulky hat, made of starched black felt, is usually avoided these days as the festivals for which the costume is worn usually involve dancing. For men, the traditional costume is a black woollen jacket with green cuffs and lapels, a red double-breasted waistcoat lined in green with gold buttons, a white shirt, black-and-white knee breeches and black buckled shoes.

cold winter. It is probably one of the most visited regions in the fjord area, largely because of the efficient Olso–Bergen railway that passes through the area, putting it on the prime tourist route. Hardanger has

something for everyone, with its tranquil lakes and valleys, strenuous mountain walks, the country's largest national park filled with native wildlife and a wealth of pretty towns and intriguing museums.

Voss

A veritable mecca for sports enthusiasts, Voss is best known as a winter ski resort *par excellence*. But there is plenty on offer in summer too, including walking, fishing, cycling or simply soaking up the sun on the shores of fjords. Sports fans flock to Voss for paragliding, kayaking and the annual extreme sports week.

The town's Vangskyrkja Church, with its beautiful painted ceiling, dates from 1277. Attractions just out of town include the 660m (2,165ft) Hanguren peak, reached via a cable car from the centre of the town for wonderful views.

102km (63 miles) east of Bergen on Highway E16.

The Norwegian fjords

Apple trees in bloom in spring at Hardanger

Voss Folkemuseum
(Voss Folk Museum)

Set amid attractive mountains, the folk museum preserves historic farm buildings and traditional crafts. Unlike many open-air museums that have relocated buildings from other towns and villages, the core of the farmsteads here are in their original location. A separate exhibition area re-creates daily life as it was in times gone by.

Mølstervegen 143.
Tel: (47) 56 51 15 11. www.visitvoss.no.
Open: mid-May–mid-Sept daily 10am–5pm; mid-Sept–mid-May Mon–Fri 10am–3pm, Sun noon–3pm. Closed: Sat. Admission charge.

MØRE & ROMSDAL

At the northern tip of fjord country, these two areas are slightly less touristy than their southern counterparts, but nevertheless contain many gems for tourists, such as the beautiful Geirangerfjord and the lovely Art Nouveau town of Ålesund.

Ålesund

The distinctive townscape of Ålesund was born out of a tragedy. At the turn of the 20th century, the town was devastated by fire, requiring the whole area to be rebuilt. The reconstruction incorporated the Art Nouveau architecture that was at that time popular in Europe, with the result that Ålesund's spires, turrets and other striking architectural details have made it one of Norway's most admired

towns. The best place to appreciate the decorative buildings is on Kongensgata. *300km (186 miles) southwest of Trondheim.*

Ålesund Museum

To get a picture of what the town looked like before the great fire and of the struggle to put out the flames, visit this museum, which also includes a model of the town. Other attractions include the innovative Brudeegget lifeboat, whose oval design became the prototype for many later boats.

Rasmus Rønnebergsgata 16.
Tel: (47) 70 12 31 70.
www.aalesunds.museum.no.
Open: Mon–Fri 11am–3pm, Sat & Sun noon–3pm. Admission charge.

Beautiful scenery at Geiranger fjord

Atlanterhavsparken
(Atlantic Sea Park)

One of the largest aquariums in Scandinavia illustrates life beneath the surface of the Atlantic Ocean. The water for the tanks is pumped in directly from the ocean through a pipeline so that the fish are actually in their natural environment. There are exhibits on all manner of oceanic activity, including fish farming, and an area devoted to shoreline kelp forests that are the habitat of lobsters, crabs and herring. At 1pm every day, visitors can watch from a viewing gallery as a scuba diver launches himself into the vast tank to feed the schools of halibut, cod, conger eel and other Atlantic fish. There are plenty of activities for children too, such as a touch pool and the opportunity to fish for crabs.
Tueneset. Tel: (47) 70 10 70 60.
www.atlanterhavsparken.no.
Open: June–Aug Sun–Fri 10am–7pm, Sat 10am–4pm; Sept–May daily 11am–4pm. Admission charge.

Jugendstilsenteret
(Art Nouveau Centre)

This explanation and demonstration centre elaborates on the roots of this architectural style and its application within Ålesund, on both building façades as well as interiors. There are also many displays of furniture and wall décor in the Art Nouveau style.
Apotekergata 16. Tel: (47) 70 10 49 70.
www.jugendstilsenteret.no.
Open: June–Aug Mon–Fri 10am–7pm,
Sat 10am–5pm, Sun noon–5pm;
Sept–May Tue–Sat 11am–4pm, Sun noon–4pm. Admission charge.

Sunnmøre Museum

This open-air museum preserves around 50 historic buildings of the region. There is also an area devoted to the history of Ålesund during the Middle Ages, when it was a centre of post-Viking Christianity. Sailing enthusiasts will enjoy the boat exhibits, which include a replica of a Viking ship.
Borgundgavlen. Tel: (47) 70 17 40 00.
www.sunnmore.museum.no.
Open: Feb–May Mon–Tue, Fri 11am–3pm, Sun noon–4pm; June–mid-Aug Mon–Fri 11am–5pm, Sun noon–5pm; mid-Aug–Sept Mon–Fri 11am–4pm, Sun noon–4pm; Oct–Dec Mon–Tue & Fri 11am–3pm, Sun noon–4pm. Closed: Jan. Admission charge.

Geirangerfjord

Beginning at the town of Geiranger, 350km (217 miles) northeast of Bergen, this beautiful 16km (10-mile) stretch of water is one of the region's most popular fjords for cruises. With its magnificent waterfalls, bearing names such as *The Seven Sisters* and *The Suitor*, and its vast mountain walls covered with deciduous forest, the area has earned a place on the UNESCO World Natural Heritage Site list. Hanging precariously over the water, as if it might crash down at any moment, the Flydalsjuvet rock is the subject of innumerable postcards.

Norsk Fjordsenter (Norwegian Fjord Centre)

Opened in 2002, this is one of the finest, if not the best, museums in the region uncovering the history of life in the Norwegian fjords, from early isolation to the area's emergence as a tourism hot spot. Exhibits illustrate different aspects such as the types of farms, from shore line to shelf farms, which were built to minimise damage from avalanches, problems with transportation and measures taken to solve them, including the creation and development of the fjord steamer, and natural disasters that have affected this region. Presented with sophistication and an emphasis on an authentic atmosphere, the displays well illustrate life along the fjords through the ages. *6216 Geiranger. Tel: (47) 70 26 30 07. www.fjordsenter.info. E-mail: booking@fjordsenter.info. Open: May & Sept daily 9am–4pm; June & Aug daily 9am–6pm; July daily 9am–10pm. Admission charge.*

Giske

An important centre during Viking times, the tiny island of Giske has a marble church dating from that era (although it was restored in the 18th century). It is also a popular sunbathing area in summer, and ornithologists will enjoy the local bird sanctuary.

Gossen

The small island of Gossen, just west of Molde, has a number of sights of interest to tourists. This was the site of several air battles during World War II, commemorated in a collection of photographs and objects from that era at the Skytterhuset in the town of Aukra. At the re-creation of a traditional working farm in the **Løvikremma Museum**, visitors can experience at first hand 19th-century agricultural life. Rindarøya has a monument commemorating a 1930s shipwreck and the bravery of those who took part in the rescue attempt. *Løvikremma Museum: Tel: (47) 71 17 30 37. Open: mid-June–July daily noon–5pm. Admission charge.*

In summer, Giske is popular with sunbathers

Hellesylt

The mountain scenery around the town of Hellesylt, 57km (35 miles) southwest of Ålesund, is particularly popular for canyoning, with the many peaks offering spectacular views of the Geirangerfjord. A waterfall flows through the heart of this small town, and fishing and boating are on offer. Nearby Norangsdalen is another valley favoured by hikers, with its deserted huts and farmhouses giving it a ghost-town feel.

Mardalsfossen

Cascading 297m (974ft) into the lake below, this stunning waterfall in the Langfjorden area can be viewed close up between mid-June and mid-August. It once flowed year round until its water was rechannelled as part of a hydroelectric project in the 1970s.

Raumabanen Railway

Running between Åndalsnes and Bjorli, this spectacular steam-train ride takes passengers past waterfalls and lakes, and over mountains and bridges, including a tunnel where the train makes a full U-turn. The most scenic part is over the Rauma River and the famous Kylling Bridge, which is floodlit at night.
www.raumabanen.com.
Operates mid-June–mid-Aug.

Runde

An island off the west coast, around 65km (40 miles) from Ålesund, Runde has one of Norway's biggest bird colonies, with a population of approximately 100,000 puffins, as well as over 200 other species of sea birds, including gannets and shags. During the nesting season, boat trips to the highly protected island are offered daily, and, if the weather is calm, boats pass through a lagoon for a closer look. The accompanying commentary gives information about the birds and the island.
www.runde.no

Sunnmøre

Looming over the vast Hjørundfjord, the imposing clifftops of the Sunnmøre Alps have drawn tourists for decades. Fishing and hiking, skiing in winter, or just relaxing near the water are the real pleasures here.

Trollstigen

Probably the most famous road in the country, the Trollstigen is a route with 11 hair-raising bends and switchbacks hacked into the mountain landscape. The best way to see this man-made feat connecting Åndalsnes and Geiranger is by either hiking or by taking a bus, when you can appreciate the wonder of the scenery without having your eyes firmly fixed on the precarious road. This is also the only place in Norway where you will see a road sign warning you of trolls. Note that the road is open to cars between May and September only.

The Norwegian fjords

Tour: The Hardanger Plateau

The drive covers 20km (12 miles), but allow a full day to include ferry trips and sightseeing.

Start at Lofthus on Highway 13.

1 Lofthus

A collection of farmsteads lines the shore at Lofthus, set in a wonderful landscape of mountains, waterfalls and orchards. Across the fjord you can catch a glimpse of the Folgefonna glacier, where summer skiing is possible. A stroll among the fruit trees is recommended at any time of year. The old stone church dating from 1250 is also worth a visit (open from 1 May to 15 September). Lofthus also boasts the tradition-rich Hotel Ullensvang and other attractions, and it is an ideal starting point for exploring the Hardangerfjord region. *Drive 10km (6 miles) north on Highway 13, along the fjord, to Kinsarvik.*

2 Kinsarvik

Kinsarvik has always been an industrial town, switching its allegiances between timber and shipbuilding, and it is still a major centre for traditional Norwegian woodcarvings. A 12th-century church is worth a look for its frescoes. *Board the car ferry for the trip to Utne.*

3 Hardanger Folkemuseum (Hardanger Folk Museum), Utne

Traditionally furnished wooden buildings spanning several periods are preserved in this impressive folk museum on the Hardanger region. Among the highlights are an exhibition about the region's famous fruit-growing success begun by Cistercian monks, an orchard of fruits no longer produced, boathouses and fishing equipment, and exhibits of

Hardanger Folkemuseum (Hardanger Folk Museum)
Tel: (47) 53 67 00 40.
www.folkemuseum.hardanger.museum.no.
Open: May–June & Sept daily 10am–4pm; July–Aug daily 10am–5pm; Oct–Apr daily 10am–3pm. Admission charge.

Eidfjord
Hardangervidda Natursenter:
Tel: (47) 53 55 59 00. Open: June–Aug daily 9am–8pm; Apr–May & Sept–Oct daily 10am–6pm. Admission charge.

Bu Museum, Ringøy
Tel: (47) 53 66 69 00. Open: June–mid-Aug, daily 11am–4pm. Admission charge.

ancient fiddles from the area, along with a fiddle-maker's workshop.
Take the car ferry to Granvin, and then drive northeast on road No 572 to Ulvik.

4 Ulvik

Birdwatchers will rejoice in the Ulvikpollen wetlands, with their large variety of avian life. Ulvik also boasts pretty rose gardens, and a wonderful crafts centre that in summer sells locally produced items.
Drive to Bruravik and take the ferry to Brimnes. Drive east along Highway 7 to Eidfjord.

5 Eidfjord

Hardangervidda, home to the country's biggest herd of wild reindeer, is Norway's largest national park. Eidfjord is a great starting point for exploring the park as it is the base for the Hardangervidda Natursenter (Hardanger Nature Centre), which explains the history of the region.
Continue east along Highway 7 to Vøringfossen.

6 Vøringfossen Waterfall

This majestic waterfall in the picturesque Måbø Valley cascades 145m (476ft) into the lake below.
From here you have the opportunity to further explore Hardangervidda park or to take a return loop back to Kinsarvik, via Ringøy.

7 Bu Museum, Ringøy

This small museum preserves three period buildings with all their original furnishings. Also included is a display of national costumes (*see p81*).

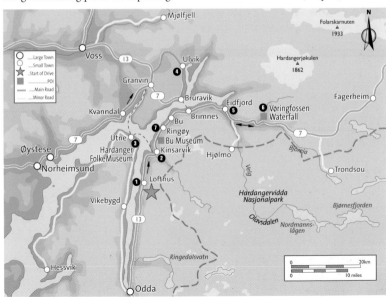

Tour: Atlantarhavsveien (the Atlantic Road)

Weaving across narrow bridges and islands, one of the most picturesque routes in Norway covers the coastal Atlantic Road between Molde and Kristiansund.

The full distance from Molde to Kristiansund covers 50km (31 miles) and will take a full day with stops to explore.

Start at Molde.

1 Molde

Molde's greatest assets, along with its jazz festival each July (*see p24*), are the breathtaking views from the peaks of the Romsdal Alps. King Håkon was forced to hide here during the German occupation in World War II, and the tree under which he reputedly sat, called the King's Birch, is now a monument. Another attraction is the open-air Romsdalmuseet (Romsdal Museum). Covering the period between the mid-18th century and around 1950, it is one of the country's largest folk museums.

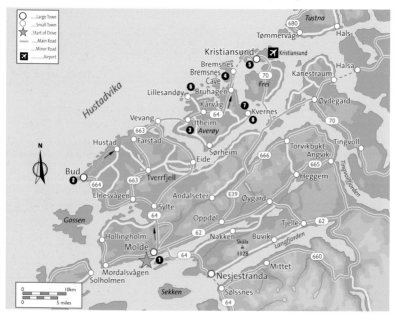

Romsdal Park. *From Molde take*
Highway 19 to Bolsøy, turn north
on road No 64, and then take road
No 664 to Bud.

2 Bud

A thriving fishing village, Bud is a
great place to stop for an early lunch
with its excellent waterfront fish
restaurants. Don't miss the fort that is
a remnant of World War II. Now
converted into a museum devoted
to the era, its highlights include
bunkers and soldiers' quarters.
Trollkirka (Troll Church) comprises
seven limestone caves, complete
with streams and a waterfall. Take
care on the often slippery rocks, and
carry a torch.
Take road No 663 to Averøy.

3 Averøy

The drive to the island of Averøy, past
the Kvitolmen lighthouse, is where the
Atlantic Road proper begins. The
landscape of tiny islands is stunning.
Continue north on road No 64 to
Bremsnes.

4 Bremsnes Cave

Archaeological evidence suggests that
the deep Bremsnes Cave was inhabited
in prehistoric and Stone Age times.

Romsdalmuseet (Romsdal Museum)
Romsdal Park. Tel: (47) 71 20 24 60.
Open: mid-June–mid-Aug daily 11am–6pm;
mid-Aug–mid-June Mon–Fri 11am–3pm; Sat
& Sun noon–3pm. Admission charge.

A marked trail guides visitors around
the cavernous interior.
From Bremsnes, you can take a ferry
straight to Kristiansund, but if there is
time, take in the small islands offshore
(see 6, 7 and 8 below).

5 Kristiansund

One of the most distinctive sights in
this region is the whitewashed buildings
of Kristiansund overlooking the
harbour. The town is made up of three
islands linked by bridges and tunnels.
This Atlantic town stands out due to its
reputation for fine opera with an
annual festival (*see p22*), and its love of
klippfish (dried cod), which even has
the honour of a dedicated museum.
The modern Kirkelandet Kirke church
has an innovative design and beautiful
stained-glass windows.

6 Honningsøya

Half of this tiny island faces directly
onto the ocean, while the sheltered side
faces the Norwegian mainland, where
there is a lovely harbour and
well-preserved 17th-century buildings.

7 Tingvoll

Stone-Age rock carvings, including
images of local marine life such as
dolphins, have been discovered here.

8 Ramsøya

This has one of Norway's few surviving
stave churches (*see pp98–9*) at Kvernes.
Its decorative choir dates from the
17th century.

Tour: Atlantarhavsveien (the Atlantic Road)

Vingen

The largest grouped set of petroglyphs in Europe, the rock art of Vingen dates back to 6000 BC by some estimates. Escorted tours to the site are available from June to mid-August.

450km (280 miles) northeast of Bergen.

NORDFJORD

The sheer tempestuousness of the Nordfjord area offers the widest variety of scenery in the fjord region, with glaciers, cascading waterfalls, lush mountains covered with flowers, and calm turquoise-blue lakes. The area thus offers a wide range of activities, from summer skiing to white-water rafting to a pony trek on the region's renowned fjord horses.

Jostedalsbreen Nasjonalpark (Jostedalsbreen National Park)

Covering an area of 487sq km (188sq miles) and spreading its tongues out into many neighbouring regions, the Jostedalsbreen ice cap is Europe's largest mainland glacier. Protected under national park status since 1991, it boasts a spectacularly varied landscape, from green agricultural valleys, rivers and waterfalls to icy peaks. The vegetation consists largely of pine forests and other hardy shrubland, while the wildlife includes brown bear, elk and deer.

Two of the park's most popular areas are Briksdalsbreen and Nigardsbreen. An enchanting way to visit the Briksdalsbreen glacier is on horse-drawn carts, which go over bridges crossing gushing waterfalls and past the glistening lakes formed by glacial waters. One of the Jostedalsbreen glacier's tongues, Nigardsbreen, can be explored on foot on a guided tour (with all the necessary safety equipment) during the summer months, which is a fantastic

Nordfjord is covered with mountains and clear blue lakes

Briksdalsbreen at the Jostedalsbreen National Park

opportunity to explore the glacial landscape at close hand. At one time there were road tracks over the glacier, but the slopes have become too precarious ever since the glacier began to shrink. The park is perennially popular with experienced hikers and walkers, and there are campsites outside the park and cabins within.
www.jostedal.com

**Jostedalsbreen Nasjonalparksenter
(Jostedalsbreen National Park Centre)**
Within the national park, this information centre explains the formation of the ice cap and the scientific research that continues to monitor it, an insight into the wildlife of the region, and a widescreen film featuring the glistening beauty of the glacier. There is also a botanical garden, focusing mainly on mountain flora. For those wishing to walk or hike in the park, the centre offers comprehensive information about the various walking routes and the equipment needed.
6799 Oppstryn. Tel: (47) 57 87 72 00.
www.jostedalsbre.no.
Open: May–Sept daily 10am–5pm.
Admission charge to exhibits.

Kråkenes Fyr
Near the large fishing port of Måløy is one of Norway's well-known ocean landmarks, Kråkenes Fyr lighthouse. With wonderfully expansive views out to sea, it offers guided tours and even overnight stays, which make for an unforgettable experience and give an insight into the life of lighthouse keepers of old.
Raudeberg. Tel: (47) 57 85 55 27.
Email: tbickhar@online.no

**Nordfjord Folkemuseum
(Nordfjord Folk Museum)**
Another of Norway's ubiquitous open-air museums, the Nordfjord Folk Museum preserves a collection of 22 old buildings, including an open-hearth cottage, smoke-oven rooms, lofts and an old school cottage.
Gota 16, Sandane (132km/82 miles south of Ålesund). Tel: (47) 57 86 61 22.
www.nordfjord.no. Open: mid-May–mid-Sept Mon–Fri 9am–4pm except July–mid-Aug Mon–Sat & Sun 1–4pm. Admission charge.

Ruins of the monastery in Selje

Selje

On the remote island of Selje, 135km (84 miles) south of Ålesund, is a monastery constructed in AD 1100. Here, sailors would take refuge from storms and pray for their safety on the area's rocky waters. The Benedictine monastery is now in ruins, but still offers an evocative impression of the isolated life of this religious order. Legend has it that the monastery was built in honour of St Sunniva, the patron saint of western Norway. Having fled her native Ireland to avoid an arranged marriage, Sunniva and her brother settled in Selje but soon came under attack from resident Vikings. However, they were saved from the Vikings by a landslide that blocked the entrance to the cave in which they lived. Some years later the cave was reopened, and Sunniva's body was found in such a pristine state that it was considered a miracle, and she was canonised.

Stryn Sommerskisenter (Stryn Summer Ski Centre)

One doesn't always need to don woollies and hats to enjoy a spot of skiing. At Stryn's summer ski centre, where there is snow all year round, skiers have been known to hit the slopes dressed only in swimwear.
146km (91 miles) south of Ålesund. Tel: (47) 57 87 54 74.
www.strynefjellet.com

SOGNEFJORD

Undoubtedly one of the world's most magnificent natural sights, Norway's longest (204km/127 miles) and deepest fjord should not be missed. The area is conducive for both a holiday full of activities as well as an ideal relaxation spot, with plenty of cultural attractions to enhance either option.

Balestrand

Balestrand has attracted a stream of artists to its picturesque setting since the 19th century, many of whom return each summer to exhibit and sell their work. Much of the pleasure of a visit here is to simply take in the laid-back atmosphere. The town also has a sense of Viking history, with an old burial mound and statues of two Viking kings.
200km (124 miles) northeast of Bergen.

Fjærland

Set in a stunning landscape of mountains and glaciers, this small, rather isolated town has become a centre for artists and bookworms. Famous as Norway's first 'book town', Fjærland has 12 shops, housed in old barns and boatyards, which sell only books in a range of languages. A small museum is devoted to the works of Nicolai Astrup (1880–1928), the well-known landscape painter.
260km (162 miles) northeast of Bergen.

Norsk Bremuseum (**Norwegian Glacier Museum**)

Everything you ever wanted to learn about glaciers, including the evolution of the fjord landscape, is fully explained here. Visitors can also go on guided tours of the Jostedalsbreen glacier (*see pp90–91*), available on request. Of more interest to most visitors to the museum, however, are the finds that have been unearthed in the region, including a mammoth's tusk. There is also an exhibition dedicated to a 5,000-year-old human corpse which

The Norwegian fjords

Night in Fjærland

was preserved in a glacier, named Ötzi.
Fjærland. Tel: (47) 57 69 32 88.
www.bre.museum.no.
Open: daily June–Aug 9am–7pm;
Apr–May & Sept–Oct 10am–4pm.
Admission charge.

Flåm

A major gateway into the Sognefjord region, Flåm is crowded all year round with hordes of tourists who descend onto the railway platform here and catch their first sight of fjord scenery from the town's picturesque harbour. The town itself doesn't have a great deal to offer other than a few hotels, souvenir shops and a shockingly overpriced canteen-style restaurant. The main reason to visit here is to experience a trip on the famed Flåm Railway and to board a ferry for a leisurely ride down the fjord.
173km (107 miles) east of Bergen.

Flåmsbana (Flåm Railway)

Clinging to steep slopes on its grafted track and passing through 20 wooden tunnels cut through the mountains to rise to a height of 900m (2,953ft), this short train ride between Flåm and Myrdal rates as one of the most spectacular in Europe. The atmosphere on the train can be a bit frenetic during the high season, when tourists react to every viewpoint indicated over the intercom by the driver, and rush to take pictures; it is far more relaxing to just sit back and take in the scenery. Trains do the 20km (12-mile) run at regular intervals.
www.flaamsbana.no.
Daily departures.

Florø

This former herring-fishing town makes for a pleasant stop on the Hurtigruten route, if only to be able to say you have visited the

Old railway carriages now serve as a café in Flåm

A remote cabin at Jotunheimen National Park

most westerly town in Norway. It is a convenient place from which to visit the rock paintings site at Vingen (*see p90*).

Sogn og Fjordan Kystmuseet (Sogn and Fjordan Coastal Museum)

The highlight of this interesting museum is a re-creation of a fisherman's family home from the turn of the 20th century. Complete with authentic furniture and furnishings, it offers a fascinating insight into the lifestyle of this coastal region in days gone by. Other exhibits explore the herring industry that has been so important to the country, and the oil industry that now dominates the economy of the region.
Florø. Tel: (47) 57 74 22 33.
Open: June–Aug Mon–Fri 10am–6pm,
Sat & Sun noon–4pm.
Admission charge.

Geilo

Norway has a great many ski resorts, but Geilo is among its most popular for both downhill and cross-country runs. It is also a thriving outdoor centre in summer, with marked trails through the mountain landscape as well as horse-riding paths.
250km (155 miles) east of Bergen.

Gulatinget

This island off the west coast has a history going all the way back to the Norse era when local assemblies were held here to determine legal matters. Today, an amphitheatre stages evocative theatre performances in summer.

Jotunheimen National Park

A haven for hikers and, in particular, mountaineers, this extensive national park features Norway's highest mountains, with Mount Galdhøpiggen topping them all at 2,469m (8,100ft). Cutting across the park is the country's first official national scenic route and the highest mountain road in Scandinavia, Sognefjell Road, which links Lom and Lustrafjord. Affording spectacular views of glaciers, mountains, waterfalls, waterside villages and farms, a drive along this road is bound to be a highlight of any holiday in the region. The road is closed during the winter months.

Lærdal

Lærdal's Lærdalsøyri area is a protected centre of 18th- and 19th-century village houses, and is also a good place to buy local handicrafts.
210km (130 miles) northeast of Bergen.

Borgund

Dating from 1180, Borgund's stave church is among the most revered, and certainly the most visited, in the country (*see p99*). Its visitors' centre, which opened in 2005, gives detailed explanations of the history and construction of stave churches.
Borgund, Lærdal. Tel: (47) 57 66 81 09. Open: daily May–mid–June & mid-Aug–Sept 10am–5pm; mid-June–mid-Aug 8am–8pm. Admission charge.

Norsk Villakssenter (**Norwegian Wild Salmon Centre**)

Salmon-fishing is a major industry in Norway, as well as a very popular recreational sport, and this centre along the Lærdal River examines the whole process, from catching the fish to exporting it to markets around the world. It also studies the mysterious life of the salmon itself, such as its migratory habits and its ability to return to the river of its birth. There is a large salmon tank to see the fish at close range, displays on creating the ideal salmon fly, and a simulator for visitors to fish for their own salmon.
6886 Lærdal. Tel: (47) 57 66 67 71. www.norsk-villakssenter.no. Open: May–Sept, daily 10am–5pm. Admission charge.

Nærøyfjord

Extending 17km (11 miles) in length but only 250m (820ft) wide at its narrowest stretch, Nærøyfjord is one of the most dramatic stretches of the Sognefjord region, and has been designated a UNESCO World Natural Heritage Site. Cruises past awe-inspiring mountain peaks and waterfalls are available between May and September.

Urnes

The oldest surviving stave church in the country, the 800-year-old church at Urnes is famed for the carvings of animals on its exterior. These are a clear indication of the transition between pagan and Christian religion in the country at this time (*see pp98–9*). The church is a UNESCO World Heritage Site.

235km (146 miles) northeast of Bergen. Urnes stave church: Tel: (47) 57 67 88 40. Open: June–Aug daily 10.30am–5.30pm. Admission charge.

Vikøyri

The main attraction of the small town of Vikøyri is the early 12th-century stave church at Hopperstad. One of the country's most appealing churches, it was renovated in the 1880s, along the lines of the area's other surviving stave churches; the roof, for instance, is reminiscent of the church at Borgund.

170km (106 miles) northeast of Bergen. Hopperstad stave church: Open: mid-May–mid-Sept daily 10am–5pm. Admission charge.

The fjord crossing at Lærdal

Norway's stave churches

One of the most distinctive aspects of the southern Norwegian landscape, particularly in the Sognefjord region, is the wooden stave churches. During the Middle Ages, King Håkon 'the Good', who had been brought up in England and therefore converted to Christianity, returned to his native Norway to rule the nation following the decline of the Vikings. In turn, he converted his nation, and the Norwegians made abundant use of their native forests to build some 1,000 wooden churches across the south of the country. Many other northern European countries also followed this technique, but strangely it is only in Norway that any still survive.

Construction of stave churches ended in the 14th century, probably because their design was no longer able to accommodate the steady growth of worshippers in each locale.

The word 'stave' refers to the method of construction. Vertical wooden posts were placed between a ground-level sill, resting on rocks, and an upper wall plank. The sill bases prevented the wood from rotting

Exterior of a stave church, Dalen

Stave church interior at Telemark

such as dragons and sea serpents. The latter addition proves that, despite its Christianisation, the country still held dear its pagan origins, a fact that can still be seen today in the Norwegian love of myths and legends (see pp100–101). Many of the churches are brightly painted inside, in particular with *rosemaling* (rose paintings).

Today, fewer than 30 stave churches survive, but some continue as places of worship, such as those at Lom in east central Norway (see p106), and Aurland in the Sognefjord region. Two have been relocated to heritage museums, such as the one at the Norsk Folkemuseum in Oslo (see pp38–9). The oldest surviving stave church, dating from 1130, is at Urnes, also in the Sognefjord district (see p96). Both its age and its beautifully intricate wood-carvings (which are thought to have been transferred here from an older church) have earned the Urnes church a place in the UNESCO World Cultural Heritage Site list. Perhaps the most famous church, and the best preserved, is however in Borgund (see p96), not least because it is on the major fjord tourist route and postcards of its picturesque exterior abound in southern Norway. All the churches are today protected by local conservationist groups.

from damp ground, which was the fate of earlier churches in the 11th century. The posts were then connected by vertical beams (staves) to form the framework of walls. All of Norway's stave churches follow this building structure, irrespective of other interior or exterior differences in design. Inside are usually a nave and a chancel, although some of the more complex churches also included an apse, or a central mast to support a spire. The other distinctive exterior feature is the pitched or gabled roof, or, in some cases, tiers of roofs. Carved or painted doorways are also a regular feature, illustrating biblical or, more commonly, mythical motifs,

Norway's trolls & other myths

The myth of Norwegian trolls goes back to pagan days, when survival within this harsh landscape necessitated a belief in natural rulers who could make or break a harvest. In other words, the better you treated the land, the better it treated you. People of those ancient times also had little understanding of the processes by which landscapes are created by natural force, and Norway's many glaciers and eroded rock formations were attributed to angry beings wresting revenge on those who crossed them.

The belief was that trolls vary widely in appearance and nature: some are gigantic and some tiny; some are friendly, some not. However, they all have certain features in common: crooked noses, four digits on each hand and foot, unruly hair reminiscent of scrubland, and a generally dishevelled look. Trolls haunt the land only at night. The many troll figures that can be seen around the country today hark back to the legend that trolls turn to stone if exposed to the sun. Their powers are supernatural, but if their land is respected they can engender good fortune.

As with most supernatural legends the world over, the threat of the trolls was often used to enforce morals and good behaviour at a time when there was little common polity. One myth, for example, explains that dirty humans are inhabited by dirty trolls, an early indication of the importance of cleanliness expressed through superstition. The *huldra* myth is related to marriage: the *huldra* is a beautiful troll who lures men into marriage, but if mistreated after the wedding, she will turn hideously ugly and make the husband's life miserable. Men were thus enjoined to treat their women well in case they uncovered a latent *huldra* in their midst.

Most trolls are said to have crooked noses and a generally dishevelled appearance

Haugfolket are pixies who hide from humans. They work the land just as humans do, but can be mischievous if annoyed. It was these folk people that formed the basis for Ibsen's famous play *Peer Gynt* (*see pp24–5*). Edvard Grieg's music composition for the play has come to symbolise the 'sound' of the Norwegian landscape, with pieces entitled the *March of the Trolls* and *Hall of the Mountain King*.

The *nisse*, similar in appearance to Father Christmas but smaller, lives on farms and looks after the livestock and the crops, as long as he himself is well looked after by the farmholders. Many farmers still follow the tradition of leaving a bowl of porridge for him at Christmas in their barns.

It is believed that trolls turn to stone if they are exposed to sunlight

Of course, Norway is a land of water as well as mountains, and various sea creatures were believed to exist in this subaquatic world. Similar to Scotland's Nessie, Selma is a supposed sea monster said to inhabit the Seljordvatn lake in southern Norway. Draugen, on the other hand, is a water ghost who wails when someone is in danger of drowning. Fossegrimen is a waterfall fiddler, who offers to teach others how to play in return for food, possibly referring to the need to keep the rivers full of fish. The *nokken* (water sprites) are said to lure people into the water, indicating the need to take care when close to the water's edge.

A great many of the images and stories, particularly of trolls, that infiltrate the modern mind-set were as much derived from the fairy tales of Asbjørnsen and Moe as from Ibsen. Illustrated with drawings by Erik Werenskiold in the 19th century, these tales are as classic for Norwegians as Hans Christian Andersen stories are for Danes. The two authors travelled the length and breadth of the country, picking up stories from local people and recording them on paper, and it is largely because of their efforts that so many of the legends survive today.

Central Norway

What can be described as central Norway is the region between the southern bulge that makes up the fjords and the two major cities, Oslo and Bergen, and the narrow strip in the north, facing the Arctic Circle. It is a landscape of beautiful national parks, a haven for winter-sports lovers, and, way up in the Lofotens, an idyllic island-hopping setting.

EAST CENTRAL NORWAY
Dombås

The small town of Dombås draws winter-sports addicts from all around, as well as cyclists in summer, but it is primarily a family destination, with its main attraction being a child-oriented theme park.

Musk ox at Dovrefjell National Park

160km (99 miles) northwest of Lillehammer.

Dovregubbens Rike Trollpark

Trolls are the mythical mountain goblins who still occupy the hearts and minds of many Norwegians (*see pp100–101*), and this theme park details those of the Dovrefjell region, including the Mountain King. The trolls and their wilderness landscape are evocatively brought to life.
N-2660 Dombås. Tel: (47) 61 24 13 33. www.trollpark.com. Open: June–Aug Mon–Fri 10am–7.45pm, Sat 10am–6.45pm, Sun 11am–6.45pm; Sept–May Mon–Fri 10am–4pm, Sat 10am–2pm. Admission charge.

Dovrefjell Nasjonalpark (Dovrefjell National Park)

Primarily a habitat for musk ox, this small but important national park is also home to Arctic foxes, wolverines and many other species. A kind of long-haired cross between a bull and a ram,

the musk ox generally inhabits Arctic regions, and has been protected in Norway since the 1930s. Guided safaris can be taken to make the most of the opportunity of seeing these rare animals in the wild. The park also offers particularly good and picturesque hiking trails.
175km (109 miles) northwest of Lillehammer.

Elverum

The centre of Norway's timber industry, the forested landscape of Elverum is today a magnet for anglers, hunters (moose abound here) and nature lovers. It also has an important place in history. It was here that King

Håkon went into exile when his country was occupied by the Germans during World War II.
85km (53 miles) southeast of Lillehammer.

Norsk Skogmuseum (Norwegian Forestry Museum)

This excellent museum has plenty of exhibits on the forestry industry, including sawmills and more ancient logging and trapping equipment. Also included are reconstructions of habitats for wildlife such as elk, and an aquarium focusing on freshwater fish such as char. Adjacent to this, the Glomdal Museum features re-creations of historic buildings from the area.

Central Norway

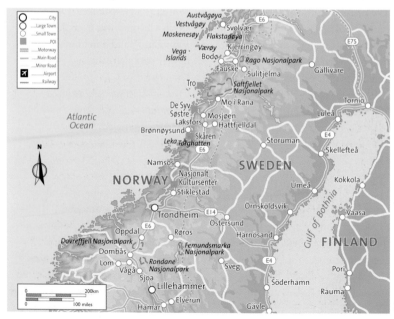

Solørveien 151. Tel: (47) 62 40 90 00.
www.skogmus.no. Open: July–mid-Aug
daily 10am–6pm; mid-Aug–June
10am–4pm. Admission charge.

Femundsmarka Nasjonalpark (Femundsmarka National Park)

The majority of Norway's reindeer are now semi-domesticated, particularly by the Sami (see p18), but in this park bordering Sweden, these graceful animals run wild in a habitat that they share with the musk oxen and the Arctic fox. This is also a popular area for the sport of falconry. The large lake that occupies much of the park is plied by a ferry: a peaceful and convenient way to take in the extended landscape.

Hamar

The lakeside setting of Hamar was the scene of several Olympic events in 1994. Designed to resemble a Viking ship and voted by Norwegians as the 'building of the century', the sports stadium still stands as a city landmark and a reminder of those glorious days.
60km (37 miles) southeast of
Lillehammer.

Norwegian Emigrant Museum

Considering its low population to begin with, emigration of Norwegians to other countries, beginning in the early 19th century, has always been a major issue for the country. Genealogical research, therefore, catering to Norwegians abroad searching for their Nordic roots or Norwegians searching for relatives overseas, is a major industry.

This museum explores the effects of emigration, retaining (or abandoning) of Norwegian traditions in their new home, the return to the motherland for many, and the personal experiences through the process.
Åkershagen. Tel: (47) 62 57 48 50.
www.museumsnett.no/emigrantmuseum.
Open: Tue–Fri 9am–3.30pm.
Admission charge.

Norsk Jernbanemuseum (Norwegian Railway Museum)

Norway's mountainous landscape did not readily lend itself to railway construction, and this interesting little museum uncovers some of the difficulties that early railway pioneers had to confront. On display are also locomotives from the late 19th century and other historic railway paraphernalia.
Strandveien 163. Tel: (47) 62 51 31 60.
www.norsk-jernbanemuseum.no.
Open: July–mid-Aug daily
10.30am–5pm; mid-Aug–June
10.30am–3.30pm. Admission charge.

Lillehammer

The town of Lillehammer really came into public consciousness as the setting for the Winter Olympics of 1994, but it had long been a skiing paradise. For those not chained to the slopes, however, there are plenty of other attractions in the town itself. In summer, white-water rafting and

mountain biking are popular activities in the surrounding area.
185km (114 miles) north of Oslo.

Lillehammer Kunstmuseum (Lillehammer Art Museum)

Containing the works of some of Norway's most acclaimed artists, including Edvard Munch and J C Dahl, the town's art museum is worth a visit.
Stortorget 2. Tel: (47) 61 05 44 60. www.lillehammerartmuseum.com. Open: mid-June–mid-Aug daily 11am–5pm; mid-Aug–mid-June Tue–Sun 11am–4pm. Admission charge.

Maihaugen Folk Museum

The Norwegians (and Scandinavians in general) are very fond of preserving their heritage in the most authentic way, by re-creating landscapes of olden days in open-air settings. Considered one of the best, Lillehammer's version has farm buildings, a stave church and various other reconstructed buildings from around the area to step back in time. Museum staff parade the grounds in period costume and explain the heritage of the exhibits.
Maihaugveien 1. Tel: (47) 61 28 89 00. www.maihaugen.no. Open: mid-May–Sept daily 10am–5pm; Oct–mid-May Tue–Sun 11am–4pm. Admission charge.

Norsk Kjøretøy-Historisk Museum (Norwegian Museum of Historic Vehicles)

As its name suggests, Lillehammer's transport museum uncovers the history of wheeled transportation in the difficult Norwegian landscape, from snow-sturdy sleighs to car production in the early 20th century, including the 1950s Troll car. Authentic backdrops and models costumed according to the cars' periods add to the appeal.
Lilletorget 1. Tel: (47) 61 25 61 65. Open: mid-June–mid-Aug daily 10am–6pm; mid-Aug–mid-June Mon–Fri 11am–3pm, Sat & Sun 11am–4pm. Admission charge.

Olympiapark (Olympic Park & Norwegian Olympic Museum)

The park encompasses the venues developed for the 1994 Winter Olympics. Just north of the town, on the Bobsleigh and Luge Track, extreme sport fans can have the thrill of a lifetime by taking a high-speed bobsled ride accompanied by an experienced guide. In summer, wheelbobs are used instead of the winter ice bob. Speeds can

The 12th-century church at Lom

reach up to 100km/h (62mph). The ski-jumping area has a chairlift up to an observation terrace where you can watch daredevil ski jumpers in action, while the ski stadium boasts a floodlit 5km (3-mile) track. Tobogganing is on offer at the Kanthaugen Freestyle Arena in winter. Housed in the stadium that held the ice hockey championships during the 1994 Winter Olympics, the Olympic Museum is dedicated to the history of the games, from its ancient origins to the present day.
Tel: (47) 61 05 42 00.
www.olympiaparken.no.
Norwegian Olympic Stadium: Håkons Hall, Lillehammer. Tel: (47) 61 25 21 00.
www.ol.museum.no. Open: June–Aug daily 10am–6pm; Sept–May Tue–Sun 11am–4pm. Admission charge.

Lom

A popular destination for hikers, with numerous marked trails in the area, Lom also boasts an original 12th-century stave church (*see pp98–9*). *178km (111 miles) northwest of Lillehammer.*

Fossheim Steinsenter

Budding geologists will certainly not want to miss Lom's most interesting museum, set in an old log barn, which displays rocks and minerals from Norway and around the world. Included in the collection is thulite, the national stone.
N-2686 Lom. Tel: (47) 61 21 14 60.
www.fossheimsteinsenter.no.
Open: daily 10am–7pm.
Admission charge.

A view of mountains at Oppdal

Oppdal

The *raison d'être* of Oppdal is winter sports; skiers and snowboarders flock here during the winter months to tackle its challenging slopes. However, there is plenty to do in the summer months as well, from gentle hikes to exciting white-water rafting trips.
222km (138 miles) north of Lillehammer.

Rondane Nasjonalpark (Rondane National Park)

Norway's first national park is one of the country's major hiking terrains, with innumerable marked trails of varying difficulty, several leading to glaciated mountains. The three mountain ranges, dominated by the Rondane massif, reach a height of 2,000m (6,562ft). Cross-country skiing is also popular in the region.
160km (99 miles) northwest of Lillehammer.

Røros

Now preserved as a UNESCO World Heritage Site, Røros came into being as a copper-mining centre in the 17th century. Legend has it that a wild reindeer first discovered the copper while kicking about in the dirt. The wooden buildings lining the town's street have been protected for their original architecture, as have the miners' homes and the slag heaps. Dating from the 18th century, the town's church features paintings commemorating various mine owners.
160km (99 miles) southeast of Trondheim.

A log house in Røros

Røros Museum

Set in a reconstructed interpretation of the original mine headquarters, this is where you can learn all about the town's mining past. Mining equipment and processes are all examined in depth.
Malmplassen. Tel: (47) 72 40 61 70. www.museumsnett.kulturnett.no/ museumsguiden. Open: daily 10am–5pm. Admission charge.

Sjoa

Northwest of Lillehammer, the Sjoa region is Norway's centre for white-water rafting, with trips available in different classes. The classic trip is a 14km (9-mile) hurl through the beating waters of the canyon, but braver souls can take the Åmot Falls route, which involves swimming in the rapids as well as plunging down cliffs. All equipment

is provided, and a sauna is available at the end of the trip.
www.sjoaadventure.com

Vågå

With pine forests, rivers and lakes, the spectacular mountainous landscape around Vågå draws hikers from all over the world. Within the town itself, the most important landmark is its 12th-century stave church (reconstructed in the 17th century), with original stonework and font. Some 150 other historic farm buildings are also now protected by a preservation order.
254km (158 miles) southeast of Ålesund.

TRØNDELAG

Located at the heart of the Trøndelag region, Trondheim is Norway's most important northern city. Surrounding it is a region largely dominated by the timber industry, making ample use of the abundant forest land.

Leka

Making for a pleasant day trip, this small offshore island is notable for its relics of the Viking era, including burial mounds at Herlaugshaugen and cave rock art. Deep within the Solsem cave, for instance, are 21 paintings of oddly shaped human figures, discovered in 1912.
335km (208 miles) north of Trondheim.

Namsos

Two words sum up Namsos: timber and moose. The town was established in the

NORWAY'S PATRON SAINT

One of the most powerful rulers Norway has seen, King Olav II Haraldsson (1015–28) was converted to Christianity while growing up in England. But his attempts to convert his compatriots and create a church state met with opposition from the aristocracy, who forced Olav into exile by supporting the invading Danes. He returned in 1030, but was slain at the Battle of Stiklestad. After his death, however, the Danish King Knut lost favour with the Norwegians, and on his death in 1035, Olav's son Magnus ascended the throne. Olav was beatified a year after his death, but was officially canonised only in 1888. During the Middle Ages, a cult of St Olav began to emerge, and a pilgrimage route was established from Oslo to the Nidaros Cathedral in Trondheim, where Olav is buried. The route goes past historic monuments in beautiful settings.

19th century as a timber-producing town, and wild moose (elks) roam the surrounding forests that generated the industry. The best view of the coastal town and the fjord is from its mountain backdrop, called Klompen, which also shelters old bunkers that were put up during World War II.

An unusual and fun activity here is to ride hired trolley cycles on the abandoned train tracks through the countryside and along the waterfront.
194km (121 miles) north of Trondheim.

Trondheim

Norway's third-largest city, Trondheim has been thriving since the Middle Ages, and is still a vibrant and attractive place to visit. In the 12th century, the city served as Norway's capital, and its importance to the nation is illustrated by the monarchy's connection to the Nidaros Cathedral. The wide range of architectural gems preserved in the Old Town area includes the 18th-century warehouses lining the canal in Bryggen, similar to those in Bergen. Above the town is a 17th-century fort, which stood firm against invading Swedes in 1718 and today offers the best aerial view of the waterfront.

Nidaros Domkirke (Nidaros Cathedral)

Possibly Norway's most important church and where royal coronations take place, the Nidaros Cathedral was built in the 11th century over the burial site of St Olav (*see box opposite*). The largest surviving medieval building in the country, the Gothic and Romanesque cathedral was reconstructed after a devastating fire in the 16th century. Several elements of the original church, such as the stonework, remain intact.

Norway's crown jewels are displayed here in summer. Next door, in the Archbishop's Palace, is a museum dedicated to the history of the cathedral. *Kongsgårdsgata 2. Tel: (47) 73 89 08 00. www.nidarosdomen.no. Open: daily. Admission charge.*

Ringve Musikkhistorisk Museum (Museum of Music History)

This unusual and enchanting museum brings together ancient and modern musical instruments from all over the world, the more unfamiliar of which are demonstrated by the talented museum guides. In the collection are traditional Norwegian violins and a vast collection of keyboard instruments, including clavichords and harpsichords. There are also exhibits showing the invention of the instruments, and a modern section that is devoted to pop music. *Lade allé 60. Tel: (47) 73 87 02 80. www.ringve.com. Open: mid-Apr–mid-Sept daily 11am–3pm; mid-Sept–mid-Apr Sun 11am–4pm. Admission charge, free Nov–Dec.*

Stiftsgården

Originally built for a local aristocrat, this 18th-century Baroque-style wooden palace is still used by the Norwegian royal family as a royal residence. Some of its 140 rooms are

The Organ Room at the Ringve Musikkhistorisk Museum

Stone carving on Nidaros Domkirke in Trondheim

open to the public, offering a wonderful insight into wealthy Norwegian life over the past three centuries.
Munkegata 23. Tel: (47) 73 84 28 80.
Open: June–Aug Mon–Sat 10am–5pm,
Sun noon–5pm. Admission charge.

Sverresborg Trøndelag Folkemuseum (Trøndelag Folk Museum)

Farmsteads, a stave church, Norway's first brick building, an old market square and other structures spanning the centuries have been relocated here from around the region. A museum on the same site is devoted entirely to the history of skiing in Norway.
Sverresborg Allé. Tel: (47) 73 89 01 00.
www.sverresborg.no.
Open: June–Aug daily 11am–6pm;
Sept–May Mon–Fri 11am–3pm,
Sat & Sun noon–4pm.
Admission charge.

Stiklestad

A landmark event in Norwegian history occurred at Stiklestad in 1030. At that time, Norway was still under the sway of feudal chieftains who opposed the Christianisation of the country under the influence of King Olav (*see p108*), defeating him here in a battle. Olav was subsequently canonised, and is still a focus for pilgrims today. A cultural centre in the town documents the importance of the battle, which is considered to have brought an end to pagan worship in Norway. The town's 12th-century church is purportedly built on the site where Olav was slain.
100km (62 miles) northwest of Trondheim on Highway E6.

NORDLAND

A buffer region between the southern fjords and northern Norway proper,

Nordland offers tranquil offshore islands, wild national parks, and the chance to cross the border into the Arctic Circle, a fact exploited by various theme-related tourist activities.

Bodø

Due to its location, Bodø is more or less the heart of the Nordland region, and thrives on the fishing industry off its coastal waters. With a wonderful setting in the Salten region and some interesting sights, it is a good stopping-off point for visitors planning to head for the northern region.

Norsk Luftfartsmuseum (Norwegian Aviation Museum)

This state-of-the-art high-tech museum grabs your attention as soon as you catch sight of its gleaming glass façade. Inside, the history of aviation, from early ambitions to modern-day jets, is covered in great detail. There is a special section on military aircraft, including displays of Spitfire and Mosquito jets, as well as a flight simulator that allows visitors to fly a Harrier jet, which is probably every young boy's dream.

Olav V gate. Tel: (47) 75 50 78 50.
www.luftfart.museum.no.
Open: mid-June–mid-Aug daily 10am–6pm; mid-Aug–mid-June Mon–Fri 10am–4pm, Sat & Sun 11am–5pm. Closed: Jan.
Admission charge.

Salten Museum: Nordland Museum

This traces the history of the Salten region, and displays fishing and agricultural paraphernalia, and details about the area's Sami inhabitants. A special section focuses on the town of Bodø itself.

Prinsensgate 116. Tel: (47) 75 50 35 00.
www.saltenmuseum.no.
Open: May–Aug Mon–Fri 9am–4pm, Sat & Sun 11am–4pm; Sept–Apr Mon–Fri 9am–3pm. Admission charge.

Brønnøysund

The picturesque setting of coastal Brønnøysund makes it an ideal halt en route to the north, as well as a good starting point for ferry trips to offshore islands.

373km (232 miles) north of Trondheim.

Nordland Museum, Bodø

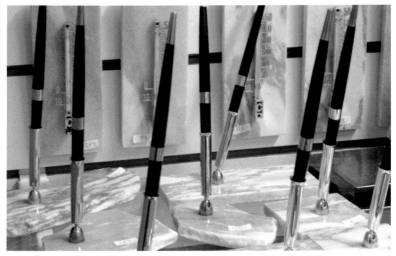
Fauske is famous for its pink marble

Hildurs Uterarium (Herbarium)
One of the more unusual features of
the area is Brønnøysund's herb garden
and shop. It not only grows some 400
different herbs but also illustrates their
uses for medicinal purposes, in cooking
and in wine-making. There's also a rose
garden and a cactus house.
Tilrem. Tel: (47) 75 02 52 12.
www.hildurs.no. Open: mid-June–
mid-Aug daily 10am–6pm.
Admission charge.

Fauske
The main claim to fame of this small
town, east of Bodø, is the pink marble
that is quarried here. Known as
Norwegian Rose, it has been exported
all over the world to decorate a range
of buildings, including the Emperor's
Palace in Tokyo, and was used on home
soil in structures such as Oslo Airport.

A small museum details the methods
of extraction and the history of this
attractive stone, and a few shops sell
locally produced marble objects.

Hattfjelldal
Numerous period buildings, such as a
forester's cottage and a 19th-century
church, have been preserved in this
small town. A cultural centre explores
the Sami heritage in the region, and
sells traditional Sami handicrafts.
381km (237 miles) northeast of Trondheim.

Kjerringøy Trading Post
North of Bodø, this open-air museum
preserves 15 buildings from the 1800s
along with their original interiors.
Among the structures are a bakery, a
general store and a manor house.

A slide show explains the history and
success of the trading post, which

began when an enterprising merchant established a connection between the value of local fish for outsiders and the locals' need for other goods.
Tel: (47) 75 50 35 05.
www.saltenmuseum.no. Open:
June–mid-Aug daily 11am–5pm.
Admission charge.

Laksforsen Waterfall

This 17m (56ft)-high waterfall gushes into the Vefsna River, which is a popular haunt of salmon fishers. The best place to watch the spectacle is from the panoramic café.
128km (80 miles) south of Mo i Rana on Highway E6.

Mosjøen

The heart of Mosjøen is the picturesque Sjøgata, a street of perfectly preserved warehouses and other buildings dating from the 18th century, including Norway's longest wooden building. One of the warehouses, Jakobsenbryggaone, houses a museum illustrating the town's history. The town also features an unusual octagonal church, built in 1735.
85km (53 miles) south of Mo i Rana on Highway E6.

Torghatten Peak

This large mound on the Trollfjord, in the Helgeland region, dominates the surrounding coastal scenery. Its distinctive feature is the 160m (525ft) hole cut through it that can be accessed by a 30-minute walk. The hole features in the Norwegian Sagas as being created by a chivalrous local trying to protect a woman's life, but in reality it was formed through centuries of climatic erosion.

The Laksforsen Waterfall

Tour: The Arctic Circle

There can be few things more enjoyable than returning home from a holiday to tell envious friends and family that part of it was spent touring the Arctic Circle. This drive takes in the border regions of the circle's demarcation lines.

Allow a full day for the approximately 160km (100-mile) route.

Start at Mo i Rana on the E6 highway.

1 Mo i Rana

With a long history as a trading post, Mo i Rana came into prominence as a mining centre in the 19th century. A museum in town traces the history of the region, and a natural history museum displays excellent exhibits detailing the geographical importance of the surrounding countryside.

Old wooden buildings recall the town's historic past. Mo i Rana is also home to the National Library of Norway.

Drive 22km (14 miles) northeast along the E6 to the Setergrotta caves.

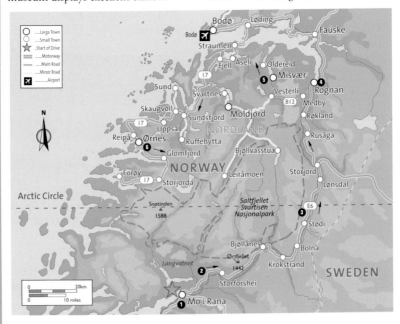

2 Setergrotta & Gronligrotta

Guided tours of these spectacular grottoes conduct visitors around marble halls, an underground river and vast caverns. The tours include equipment. *Continue north on the E6 towards Rognan.*

3 Polarsirkelsenteret (Arctic Circle Centre)

A range of attractions at this slightly tacky tourist venture marks the fact that the Arctic Circle runs through the centre. Souvenirs and various other items, including the largest stuffed polar bear in Europe, focus on the polar region. You can also send a postcard home to make your friends marvel at the Arctic Circle postmark. With a restaurant serving traditional northern Norwegian cuisine, it is also a good spot for dinner at the end of the drive.

4 Salten Museum Saltdal bygdetun og Blodveimuseet (Salten Museum and Blood Road Museum)

Just north of the town of Rognan is a museum devoted to preserving period buildings in their original state. However, of more interest here is the Blood Road Museum, which explores the fate of prisoners of war under German occupation during World War II. Nearby is Blood Road, the road the prisoners were forced to labour on and where many died, hence the name.
Continue west on the 812 road to Misvær.

Setergrotta & Gronligrotta
N-8615 Skonseng. Tel: (47) 75 16 23 50. www.setergrotta.no. Open: mid-June–mid-July guided tours daily 3pm; mid-July–mid-Aug guided tours daily 11am & 3pm. Admission charge.

Polarsirkelsenteret
Highway E6, Rognan. Tel: (47) 75 12 96 96. www.polarsirkelsenteret.no. Open: May–mid-Sept daily. Free admission.

Salten Museum Saltdal bygdetun og Blodveimuseet
N-8250 Rognan. Tel: (47) 75 50 35 31. www.saltenmuseum.no. Open: mid-June–mid-Aug daily 11am–5pm, until 8pm Thur. Admission charge.

5 Misvær

Best known for its goat's cheese, Misvær also boasts plenty of architectural highlights, with buildings preserved from the past three centuries. *Continue on the 812 to Straumen then turn south onto route 17 to Ørnes.*

6 Ørnes

Take in the sights and atmosphere of this former trading post before settling down to a picnic lunch with stunning views of the coastal landscape.

THE ARCTIC CIRCLE

The Arctic Circle is an imaginary line at a latitude of 66° 33' 38" N, beyond which is the area known as the Arctic Zone. As well as Norway, the Arctic Circle includes parts of Russia, Sweden, the USA, Canada, Finland and Greenland within its territory. Significant aspects of the Circle are the phenomena known as Midnight Sun and Polar Night. In June each year, there is a 24-hour period when the sun never sets; in turn, in December there is another 24-hour period when the sun never rises above the horizon.

Tour: The Arctic Circle

Rago Nasjonalpark (Rago National Park)

Experienced hikers searching for some untouched wilderness can do worse than make their way to Rago National Park, on the border with Sweden. The area is renowned for its icy waterfalls, deep ravines and mountain ridges.

Saltfjellet-Svartisen Nasjonalpark (Saltfjellet-Svartisen National Park)

Spreading over more than 2,000sq km (772sq miles), this large park offers numerous hiking trails, including one to Norway's second-largest glacier, Svartisen, for experienced ice walkers. An easier way to see the icecap is by boat; ferries ply the Holandsfjorden throughout the summer.
North of Mo i Rana, with trails accessed from Route 77.

Saltstraumen

Every six hours, without fail, the world's strongest maelstrom gushes through the narrow strait near Saltenfjorden at speeds of 37km/h (23mph), creating large, deep whirlpools in its wake. Apart from this spectacular phenomenon, the region's attraction is its large population of cod, halibut and other fish, which draws avid anglers from all over the country.

Skåren

Within a deep cave at Skåren, 6km (4 miles) south of Brønnøysund, rock paintings of local animals have been discovered which historians believe to be 5,000 years old. Visits are not guided, so be sure to wear suitable boots and take safety precautions.

Sulitjelma Mining Museum

This former mining community is honoured in a fascinating museum that examines not only its mining methods, but also the lives of the mining community. Having absorbed the history, don't miss a chance to visit the real thing: there are guided tours to the mine itself.
46km (29 miles) east of Bodø.
Tel: (47) 75 64 02 40. Open: daily mid-June–mid-Aug 11am–5pm; mid-Aug–mid-June 9am–3pm. Mine tours: open mid-June–mid-Aug daily 1pm. Admission charge.

De Syv Søstre (Seven Sisters Range)

Looming over the town of Sandnessjøen, to the southwest of Mo i Rana, are seven legendary peaks, reaching heights of more than 1,000m (3,281ft). A number of hiking trails lead to the summits, which offer a spectacular view of the coastline, and every year ambitious walkers take part in a contest to reach all seven summits in the fastest possible time. Sandnessjøen is also a good base for ferry trips to the neighbouring islands.

Tro

Stone Age rock carvings discovered in Tro, on the island of Rødøy, include an image that is thought to be the earliest representation of a skiing man. The motif was adapted for use as the symbol for the 1994 Winter Olympics in Lillehammer.

Vega Islands

These 6,500 islands were declared a UNESCO World Heritage Site in 2004 due to their picturesque preservation of traditional fishing villages in the Arctic zone and their economically important practice of quilt-making using down from indigenous ducks. A heritage trail uncovers the Viking history of the region.

Off the west coast, accessible by a 5-hour ferry trip from Bodø.

THE LOFOTEN ISLANDS

Reaching out from the mainland coast like a waving arm, the Lofotens are an idyllic setting for a summer holiday island-hopping, cycling, hiking and eating fresh fish. Cod-fishing (*see pp122–3*) is the livelihood for many of the inhabitants here, and their coastal way of life is charming to observe. Car ferries make regular journeys to the islands from the mainland.

Austvågøy

The most popular Lofoten island is Austvågøy, for the simple reason that it is closest to the mainland and therefore most readily accessible. But one advantage breeds another, and the

A distant view of De Syv Søstre, the seven legendary peaks

Henningsvær

concentration of tourists also results in a concentration of things to do.

Henningsvær

Contrary to popular opinion, this region of Norway generally experiences a bright and warm summer, a fact that is reflected in the numerous pavement bars and cafés looking out on to beautiful beaches and landscapes.

Svolvær

The town of Svolvær is a major hub of the Lofotens, with numerous ferry trips and excursions taking off from there. The region is also an excellent whale-watching spot between October and December, when the orca (killer) whales arrive in the area.

Lofoten Theme Gallery

A film illuminating the history of the island group, from their geographical creation to their fishing and whaling industry, is an ideal way to begin any holiday to the area. Exhibits of whaling equipment can also be seen.
Svolvær Sjøhuscamp.
Tel: (47) 76 07 03 36.
www.svolver-sjohuscamp.no.
Open: daily 10am–3pm & 6–8pm.
Admission charge.

Magic Ice

An unusual way to learn about
the region and its history is through
this collection of ice sculptures
accompanied by music and
light shows.
*Svolvær quay. Tel: (47) 76 07 40 11.
www.magic-ice.no. Open: June–Aug
noon–10.30pm; Sept–May 6am–10pm.
Admission charge.*

Svolvær Krigsminnemuseum (War Memorial Museum)

The Lofotens may seem like an
incongruous location for what is
probably the best wartime museum in
the country, but this was a region of
heavy battle during World War II.
Among the displays are uniforms and
medals from the era, as well as
fascinating photographs of the bombing
raids here.
*Tel: (47) 91 73 03 28.
www.lofotenkrigmus.no.
Open: June–Sept Mon–Fri 10am–4pm
& 6.15–10pm; May & Oct Mon–Fri
6.15–10pm. Admission charge.*

Storvågen

In the Middle Ages, impoverished
fishermen slept beneath their
upturned boats, awaiting dawn so
that they could go out to sea again and
earn their living. King Øystein rectified
the matter in the 12th century by
ordering the construction of *rorbuer*
(fishermen's huts) to shelter the men
who greatly contributed to the
kingdom's economy. Some of these
original huts can still be seen in
Storvågen on the island of Austvågøy.

Flakstadøy

Possibly the most picturesque of the
Lofotens, which is saying a lot,
considering the beauty of the area,
Flakstadøy is defined by its old-style
buildings and fishermen's huts,
particularly in the town of Nusfjord.
One of the most popular spots is
Ramberg Bay, an exquisite setting of
sandy beach flanked by ice-topped
mountains. Near Ramberg is the
18th-century Flakstad church, with
an onion-shaped dome.

Moskenesøy

For avid hikers and mountain climbers
Moskenesøy is the island to head for,
with its craggy mountain ranges rising
up out of the sea. The island's most
appealing town is Reine, with its
breathtaking landscape of a mountain
backdrop offsetting azure waters.

Norsk Fiskeværs Museum (Norwegian Fishing Museum)

Probably the most comprehensive
explanation of life in a Lofoten fishing
village, the museum is divided into 14
sections that explore the fishery
industry, the production of cod liver oil,
and *rorbuer*, among other things.
*Tel: (47) 76 09 14 88.
www.lofoten-info.no/nfmuseum.
Open: mid-June–mid-Aug daily
10am–6pm; mid-Aug–mid-June
Mon–Fri 11am–3pm. Admission charge.*

Måstad village, Værøy

Norsk Tørrfiskmuseum (Lofoten Stockfish Museum)

A Norwegian delicacy that is immensely popular in southern Europe as well as in Scandinavia is *tørrfisk* (dried cod). This small but intriguing museum explains the drying process and the many uses for the dried fish in cooking.
Tel: (47) 76 09 12 11.
www.lofoten-info.no/stockfish.htm.
Open: mid-June–mid-Aug daily 11am–6pm; mid-Aug–mid-June Mon–Fri 11am–3pm.
Admission charge.

Refsvikhula

An extraordinarily eerie sight is the 3,000-year-old rock paintings of the Refsvik cave, which are illuminated by the sun through a hole in the cavern in summer. They were discovered in 1986.

Værøy

Værøy is a paradise for ornithologists, who come here to observe the colonies of puffins, guillemots, cormorants and many other bird species that nest on the island's cliffs. Birds have played a major role in the life of the locals. At one time, inhabitants of the village of Måstad hunted puffins and cured their meat in salt, while in other areas men had been known to hunt and catch eagles with their bare hands. Today, the majority of the people are involved in fishing.

Vestvågøy

Alongside fishing, agriculture and dairy farming play an important role on this mountainous island, which is particularly known for its good-quality cheese and lamb. For tourists, white sand beaches and a multitude of hiking trails are the main draw here.

Lofotr Vikingmuseum
(Lofoten Viking Museum)

In the town of Borg, archaeologists discovered the remains of the largest Viking building in the world, dating from AD 500, and a museum was subsequently erected to preserve this big find. A reproduction of the house and a model of the Lofotr Viking ship are the highlights here, but there is a wealth of other information about the history of this great ancient clan in the region.

Borg. Tel: (47) 76 08 49 00.
www.lofotr.no. Open: May daily 11am–
5pm; June–Aug daily 10am–7pm;
1 Sept–mid-Sept daily 11am–5pm;
mid-Sept–Apr Fri 1–3pm.
Admission charge.

Lofotr Vikingmuseum, Borg

Cod-fishing in the Lofoten Islands

Thanks largely to the Gulf Stream, the waters around the Lofoten Islands have been almost consistently full of Atlantic cod, and cod-fishing has been a vital part of the islands' economy for around 1,000 years. Between January and April each year, the cod arrive in the region of their birth to spawn, making use of the relatively warm waters, good currents and abundant food supply.

Originally the first fishermen here in the 12th century snared the cod with the use of nets and hook and lines, until longlines appeared in the 16th century. However, the industry in its nascence was a fairly tumultuous affair, with fierce competition between fishermen and their methods, and no regulation. This was resolved, in theory, in 1816, when the government instigated the *Loftoloven* (Lofoten Act). This defined the water areas that each fishing village could use, and set a standard time for when fishing could begin and end each day. But in retrospect the law was ridiculous as the fish, obviously, didn't comply with the boundaries set by the government, leaving some villages with a vast amount of cod, and some with barely any. The law was repealed in 1857. But it wasn't until 1938, with the Raw Fish Act, that the situation really calmed down. The new act set a fixed price on the fish, preventing wealthy fish buyers from offering under-market prices, and allowing all fishermen to charge the same price for their catch. It put an end to the unfriendly competition and ushered in a kind of co-operative effort between the fishermen. Today, the fishermen divide the waters themselves, and each village's craft must stay strictly within their borders, unless they are fishing with simple hand-held rods.

As with most agricultural practices, income and returns can never be guaranteed, and the cod-fishing industry underwent something of a crisis in the 1980s when it seemed that the waters had been over-fished and the cod count was at an all-time low. The situation began to improve in the mid-1990s, but the locals live in constant flux and concern as they have done for centuries,

Catching fish

Cod drying

wondering whether this will be a year of profit or loss.

One of the most notable products of the Lofotens is stockfish (dried cod fish, or *tørrfisk* in Norwegian), which in early spring can be seen drying on racks. This area of fish production renders one of the most nutritious forms of fish, with all the goodness of the cod preserved but the water removed by the gradual exposure to fresh air. Vikings were thought to have begun this process, using the long-lasting preserved fish as vital food supplies during their long voyages. The dried cod is not only popular in Scandinavia but also in southern Mediterranean countries such as Portugal, Spain and Italy. Its production and export are a vital part of the Norwegian economy.

Other valuable products from the humble cod are salted cod's roe and cod liver oil, produced by boiling the fish liver. In olden days, the oil was an extremely important part of the industry as it was used in paint and soap products, as fuel and as a preventative health medicine for its high levels of Vitamins A and D. The oil production is still relevant here, but demand has reduced as advances in electricity and medical science have been made.

The cod-fishing industry has benefited the islanders in other ways as well. Because of the importance of the fish industry, the Lofoten Islands were selected as the site for Norway's first telegraph line in 1861. The reason was this new communication system would enable weather forecasts and information about the best fishing areas to be relayed to the fishermen, substantially increasing the annual yield. Just under 50 years later, this was also the location of the country's first wireless telegraph.

Everyone in Lofoten becomes involved in the winter fishing activities in some form or another. Traditionally, autumn was spent in men checking and repairing their boats and tackle while the women baked vast amounts of bread and other foodstuffs for the men to carry with them during their months of fishing. Today, with modern technology, this is not so important, but there is still a buzz in the air during the fishing season (as well as a pungent aroma). Women still work in the fish factories, tying the fish tails together, while the cutting out of cod tongues is the traditional apprenticeship of young Lofoten boys.

Northern Norway

Northern Norway primarily consists of the counties of Troms and Finnmark, although the Vesterålen Islands, north of the Lofotens, geographically fit within this area. This is no destination for city-lovers: the landscape is defined by mountains and glaciers, forests and fishing villages and, in summer, the great outdoors glimmering under the midnight sun.

The people have adapted to their unique latitude and landscape, and continue to live off the land and sea: salmon fishing and deep sea fishing here are the best in Norway. The northernmost part of the region, Finnmark, as its name suggests, stretches to the borders with Finland and Russia, incorporating all the cultural and historical factors of this multinational crossroads.

VESTERÅLEN ISLANDS
Andøya

The northernmost of the Vesterålen Islands is best known to tourists for its whale-watching potential. A major reason is the presence of giant squid in its coastal waters, which attract whales in search of food. The Whale-watching Centre in the town of Andenes gives tourists a background on the world's largest mammal, as well as a history of the whaling trade. Whale-watching trips can be booked here or at the town's tourist office.

Hadseløya

Closest to the Lofoten group, Hadseløya's claim to fame is as the birthplace of the now famous Hurtigruten ferries that ply the waters of the Norwegian coast all the way from Bergen to Kirkenes and back again (*see p27*). The service began in 1881, not only for passengers but also largely to carry much-needed supplies and communication to what were then highly remote regions. Today, with the advent of road transport, much of the service is given over to tourism. A museum in Stokmarknes traces the ferry's history.

Langøya

The main attraction of Langøya is Nyskund, not least because of its chequered history and phoenix-like ability to rise from the ashes: literally, on one occasion. A relatively successful fishing village in the 19th century, much of it was destroyed by fire in the 1930s. Although there were attempts to

Northern Norway

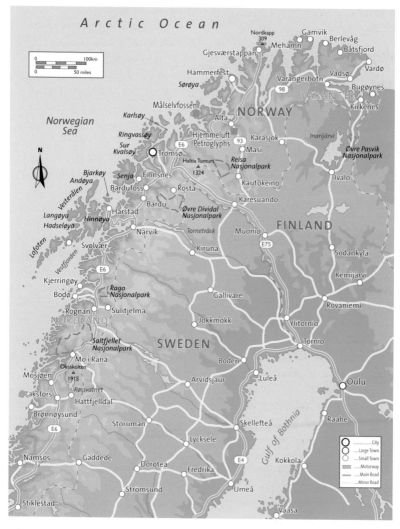

Arctic Ocean

Nordkapp 309
Gamvik
Berlevåg
Mehamn
Gjesværstappan
Båtsfjord
Hammerfest
Vadsø
Vardø
Sørøya
Varangerbotn
Bugøynes
98
VARANGER
Målselvfossen
Kirkenes
Karlsøy
Alta
NORWAY
Norwegian Sea
Ringvassøy
Hjemmeluft
Karasjok
Inarijärvi
Sur Kvaløy
Petroglyphs
93
Masi
Øvre Pasvik Nasjonalpark
Tromsø
Reisa Nasjonalpark
Haltia Tunturi 1324
Bjarkøy Andøya
Senja
Finnsnes
Kautokeino
Ivalo
Bardufoss
Rosta
Karesuando
Bardu
Harstad
Øvre Dividal Nasjonalpark
Langøya
Hinnøya
FINLAND
Hadseløya
Narvik
Torneträsk
Muonio
Vesterålen
Svolvær
Kiruna
E75
Sodankylä
Lofoten
Vestfjorden
E6
Kjerringøy
Rago Nasjonalpark
Gallivare
Kemijärvi
Bodø
Rognan
Sulitjelma
Rovaniemi
NORDLAND
Jokkmokk
Ylitornio
Saltfjellet Nasjonalpark
SWEDEN
Tornio
Mo i Rana
Oksskolten 1915
Boden
Mosjøen
Røssvatnet
Arvidsjaur
Luleå
Oulu
Laksfors
Hattfjelldal
Brønnøysund
Skellefteå
E6
Storuman
Raahe
Namsos
Gäddede
Lycksele
E4
Kokkola
Dorotea
Fredrika
Stiklestad
Strömsund
Umeå
Vaasa
Gulf of Bothnia

0   100km
0   50 miles

N

City
Large Town
Small Town
Motorway
Main Road
Minor Road

rebuild the town, the modernisation of the fishing industry worked against it and it was abandoned. For some reason the town wouldn't rest, and in the 1980s an initiative was put in place to rebuild and renovate what was there.

Today, it attracts artists and writers to its idyllic setting, and in summer has a laid-back, almost bohemian atmosphere all its own. Nyskund is also a popular tourist spot for the whale-watching opportunities it provides.

The Norwegian Sea, Troms

TROMS
Bjarkøy

For a taste of Viking heritage, don't miss the evocative island of Bjarkøy, dubbed the 'saga island'. According to legend, it is the birthplace of the Viking Tore Hund, who was later to battle King Olav at Stiklestad in the 11th century (*see p108*). There is a memorial to the great warrior on the island, as well as Viking burial sites. A small museum explains the mysterious history of the place. There is also a marked heritage trail.

Harstad

The cultural heart of Norway's largest island, Hinnøya, Harstad boasts numerous attractions. Among them are cultural centres, restored buildings, sailing trips and hiking opportunities.

North Norwegian Preservation Centre and Boat Museum

As the northernmost strip of mainland Europe, north Norway boasts a fascinating coastal history. This museum provides an insight into it, focusing on fishing and boat-building of the past 200 years in the region, as well as the skills required to preserve and restore old ships.

9470 Gratangsbotn. Tel: (47) 77 02 03 70. Open: mid-June–July daily 11am–6pm. Admission charge.

Karlsøy

Rather like Nyskund on the Vesterålen island of Langøya (*see pp124–5*), this small fishing village met with almost total decline until it attracted the interest of a bohemian community of artists, writers and general anti-establishment types in the 1980s. The values of the community are largely based on living close to nature and rejecting capitalism. Today, an annual summer festival (Karlsøyfestivalen) in August invites like-minded artists and musicians from all over the world. It might all seem a bit like harking back to 'hippie heaven', but given the abandoned state of the village only a few decades ago, it is an inspiring tale of revitalisation.

64km (40 miles) north of Tromsø.

Lyngenfjord & the Lyngen Alps

The main attraction in this region for experienced mountaineers and extreme sport skiers are the tricky alpine peaks.

Also drawn to the 150km (93-mile)-long Lyngenfjord are anglers and watersports fanatics. Rife with halibut, catfish and cod, the fjord also has wrecks of various boats, including the *Sjølv*, once used by Roald Amundsen (*see pp46–7*). Diving trips to the wrecks can be arranged.
80km (50 miles) east of Tromsø.

Målselvfossen Waterfall

Considered Norway's national waterfall, this spectacular 500m (1,640ft)-long cascade is particularly noted for its summer salmon fishing, and a 'window' viewing area has been specially constructed so that visitors can watch the 450m (1,476ft) salmon ladder as these fish ascend the fall. Trout and char fishing are also popular, and licences for both can be bought locally.

Øvre Dividal Nasjonalpark (Øvre Dividal National Park)

Spread over 740sq km (286sq miles), this park is dotted with lakes and draws plenty of nature enthusiasts for short or long hikes. One of the most popular of them has the unique feature of covering three different countries: Norway, Sweden and Finland. The pine and birch forests protect a wide range of flora and fauna, including Arctic rhododendron, brown bears, wolverine and lynx. The area is also a major habitat of the Sami people (*see p18*), and their reindeer use the park as grazing ground.

Approximately 85km (53 miles) south of Tromsø, accessed via Highway E08 and Route 87.

Reisa Nasjonalpark (Reisa National Park)

An impressive canyon crossed by the Reisa River is the backdrop for this national park, dotted with waterfalls. The greatest attraction here is the 269m (883ft) Mollisfossen waterfall, which is accessible on foot via an approximate 4-hour hike, or by boat. The landscape harbours some of the finest wildlife in the entire north, including brown bears, Arctic foxes and birds of prey, among them the golden eagle. Another significant aspect of the valley is that it is home to Sami people and Finns (Kven), and cultural heritage sites inform visitors of the mixed ethnicity of the region.

(continued on p130)

Cultural heritage site of the Sami people

Aurora borealis & the Midnight Sun

One of the most popular winter tourist attractions in Norway is the optical phenomenon known as the *aurora borealis*, commonly known as the Northern Lights. The first documented sighting of the *aurora borealis* dates back to 1250.

Aurora, deriving from the Latin word for dawn, is the term used for the optical effect of strange lights in the night sky that is caused by energy particles of solar wind interacting with the magnetic atmosphere of the Poles. (The similar phenomenon in the Southern Hemisphere is referred to as the *aurora australis*.) The lights

Midnight Sun

are at their strongest when the Earth's magnetic field is working in the opposite direction to the interplanetary magnetic field. These events, to the naked eye, take the form of 'dancing' rays and arcs of multicoloured light, at times resting still and silent, then swirling and twisting in the night sky, in hues of yellow, green, red and sometimes blue. The lights generally occur between midnight and dawn. Scientists can usually tell when particularly spectacular lights will occur by measuring the magnetic field with magnetometers.

One even stranger aspect of the lights is that many people claim the aurorae are accompanied by humming sounds, but this has never been proved scientifically. It is likely that, particularly in wide-open spaces where there are no other sounds audible, these are just the sound of the air itself. Or perhaps the lights create a sharper sense of spirituality in the observer, causing them to believe the lights are 'singing'.

Unsurprisingly, before the advent of science that could pinpoint the

Aurora borealis

physics of the phenomenon and explain their presence, the northern lights were a major topic of folklore. They were usually considered spirits, particularly of those souls trapped in purgatory, and having ominous implications.

Apart from being a sensational vision and experience, the lights are a welcome diversion for Norwegians during the period that is known as the Polar Night; in ancient times, many believed that they were actually sent by the dead to brighten the otherwise dreary dark. During this period, the sun barely raises its head, giving off, at best, a faint dusk-like haze and, at worst, a permanent night that can be depressing for long periods of time. At this time, many Norwegians are diagnosed with Seasonally Affective Disorder (SAD), a very real condition linked to the lack of Vitamin D that is derived from sunlight.

The best time to see the northern lights is from October to March, and the further north you are, the better the sightings; Tromsø (*see p130*) has built up a rather large tourist industry based around the phenomenon. Don't head for Svalbard, however, to witness this: the archipelago is too far north and the lights bypass the region altogether.

In contrast to the winter northern lights, the summer phenomenon is known as the Midnight Sun. Between May and August, particularly in the far north, the sun never sets beneath the horizon because the North Pole is tilted towards the sun on the Earth's axis at this time of year. After the long, dark winter, this is a very welcome period in Norwegian life, and many summer festivities are all-night occasions to make the most of the light.

There is a variety of marked hiking trails and a number of unstaffed cabins. Anglers and hunters (with the necessary licences) can also operate within the park.

130km (81 miles) east of Tromsø.

Trollparken (Troll Park)

This may all seem a bit kitsch, but the Norwegian obsession with trolls is very real (*see pp100–101*), and children in particular will enjoy the troll-style entertainment here, even if the sour-cream porridge served by 'wood nymphs' is not to their liking. The carving of the Senja troll, based on the figure that was thought to roam the land and sea of the area, is the largest troll image in the world, at 18m (59ft) high, and its hollow interior houses various exhibits and adventure opportunities based on the legends of the trolls.

Finnsæter, 9385 Skaland, Senja, 130km (81 miles) southwest of Tromsø.
Tel: (47) 77 85 88 64.
www.senjatrollet.no. Open: June–Aug daily 9am–9pm. Free admission.

Tromsø

The largest city in northern Norway seems to rejoice in its setting on the edge of the continent, and no more so than in summer when the months of midnight sun lead to an endless array of festivities. Buskers in the street, crowded bars and a wonderfully fresh mountain backdrop make a visit here a highlight of any trip to the region, and its status as a university town ensures a youthful vibe.

Botaniske Hage (Botanical Garden)

Tromsø's obsession (and in fact, that of the whole region) of applying the 'northernmost' tag onto almost everything can become tedious, but the city's botanical gardens are genuinely a lush miracle in this icy landscape. Unsurprisingly, the main focus is on Arctic and Alpine species, but many plants from other mountain regions, including the Himalayas, also thrive here.

Universitetsområdet, Breivika.
Tel: (47) 77 64 40 00.
www.uit.no/botanisk.
Open: May–Sept daily. Free admission.

Ishaavskatedralen

Tromsø's cathedral, often referred to as the Arctic Cathedral, is immediately striking for its 11 glistening white spires, created to emulate the jagged peaks of the region's icecaps. In a region that is plunged into darkness for so much of the year, the celebration of light is taken seriously, and here it is beautifully refracted in the stained-glass window on the cathedral's façade. In summer, Ishaavskatedralen becomes a spectacular setting for night-time concerts under the midnight sun.

Tel: (47) 77 75 35 00. Open: mid-Apr–May & mid-Aug–Sept daily 4–6pm; June–mid-Aug daily 10am–8pm; Oct–Mar Sun 4–6pm. Admission charge, free during services.

Macks Ølbryggeri (Mack Brewery)

The Mack Brewery was opened in 1877 by Louis Mack, and his descendants have continued to produce beer, including Pilsners and dark beers, for over 100 years. Tours of the brewery include a step-by-step guide to the beer-producing process and conclude with a tasting in the Ølhallen pub next door.
Storgata 5–13. Tel: (47) 77 62 45 00. www.mack.no. Open: Mon–Thur noon–4pm. Admission charge.

Nordlysplanetariat (Northern Lights Planetarium)

For obvious reasons, most people visit Tromsø in summer, but this does mean that they miss one of the area's most famous 'sights', the winter *aurora borealis* phenomenon (*see pp128–9*). Tromsø's planetarium resolves this issue by staging simulated shows of the dazzling light show.
University campus, Breivika. Tel: (47) 77 67 60 00. Open: June–mid-Aug Mon–Fri 11am–6pm, Sat & Sun 11am–4.30pm. Admission charge.

Nordnorsk Kunstmuseum (Art Museum of Northern Norway)

One of Norway's finest art museums and certainly the best in the north exhibits Norwegian art from the 19th century to the present day, with a strong accent on northern and Sami artists. Other highlights include some works by Edvard Munch, on loan from the National Gallery in Oslo.
Sjøgata 1. Tel: (47) 77 64 70 20. www.museumsnett.no/nordnorsk-kunstmuseum.

The Arctic Cathedral (Ishaavskatedralen) has striking stained-glass windows

Open: mid-May–mid-June Tue–Fri 10am–5pm & mid-June–mid-Aug Sat & Sun 10am–5pm. Admission charge.

Polaria

Set up in 1998, this high-tech science centre is immediately recognisable because of its exterior architecture resembling toppling icecaps. It offers IMAX films on the history and the geography of the region, an aquarium, a seal pool, an interactive area (largely geared towards children) and exhibits examining the region's contribution to the oil industry.

Hjalmar Johansens gata 12. Tel: (47) 77 75 01 11. www.polaria.com. Open: daily mid-May–mid-Aug 10am–7pm; mid-Aug–mid-May noon–5pm. Admission charge.

An exhibit of a ship at the Polar Museum

Polarmuseet (Polar Museum)

While Polaria focuses on the natural aspect of the polar region, this museum turns its attention to man's successes and failures in adapting to life in the Arctic. Housed in a listed 19th-century warehouse, the museum has displays on hunting, trapping, whaling and the equipment used, and details about the numerous explorative expeditions that have set out from the region.

Søndre Tollbugate 11. Tel: (47) 77 68 43 73. www.troms.kulturnett.no/pol. Open: daily July–Aug 10am–7pm; Sept–June 11am–3pm. Admission charge.

Tromsø Museum

Northern Norway's largest museum covers just about anything you would want to know about Europe's northernmost frontier, from fossils and dinosaurs to the area's current wildlife inhabitants. There are geological displays, Stone Age rock carvings, Viking buildings, an exhibition on the Sami culture, as well as an area devoted to the Northern Lights phenomenon.

Lars Thøringsvei 10, Folkeparken. Tel: (47) 77 64 50 00. www.uit.no/tmu. Open: Sept–May Mon–Fri 9am–3.30pm, Sat noon–3pm, Sun 11am–4pm; June–Aug daily 9am–6pm. Admission charge.

Tromsø Forsvarsmuseum (Tromsø Defence Museum)

Norway, and the north in particular, suffered substantially during World War II (*see p135*), and Tromsø's

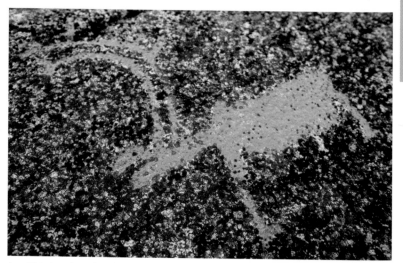

A prehistoric rock carving of a reindeer at Alta Museum

museum, which is dedicated to Norwegian resistance and defence against the German invading army, is fascinating even if you aren't into military history. Among the exhibits are the story of the sinking by the British of the German battleship *Tirpitz* near Håkøya in 1944, an old bunker, and other wartime tales and landmarks in the city.

Solstrandveien, Kaldslett.
Tel: (47) 77 62 88 36.
Open: May–Sept daily noon–5pm;
Oct–Apr Mon–Thur noon–5pm.
Admission charge.

FINNMARK
Alta

The largest city in Finnmark naturally sees its fair share of tourists, not least as a base from which to explore the area's many sights, but unlike many

convenient stop-off points Alta is not short of its own interests. Nearby is the Sautso Alta canyon, the largest in Europe, and a great hiking spot.

Hjemmeluft Petroglyphs – Alta Museum

Now designated a UNESCO World Cultural Heritage Site, these prehistoric rock carvings were first discovered in 1972 near Alta and have now been incorporated into the Alta Museum. Depicting hunting and fishing scenes, the carvings date back some 6,000 years. A series of pathways has been set up to lead visitors along the route of these fascinating petroglyphs, which offer a remarkable insight into the ritual life and landscape of the area in prehistoric times. The rest of the museum is divided into six sections focusing on, among other things,

Hammerfest harbour, dusk

the Stone Age, Sami life, the Northern Lights and the controversial local hydroelectric dam.
Tel: (47) 78 45 63 30.
www.alta.museum.no. Open: May & Sept daily 9am–6pm; June–Aug daily 8am–9pm; Oct–Apr Mon–Fri 9am–3pm, Sat & Sun 11am–4pm. Admission charge.

Bugøynes

Because of the devastation wrought by World War II on the area, very little of Finnmark's pre-war architecture has survived. Amazingly, Bugøynes escaped the mayhem. Here, original early 19th-century Finnish architecture erected by early immigrants can still be seen, in particular at Lassigården, which has former merchants' houses. Among other draws here are the Ranvika Bird Sanctuary, at the end of a 90-minute marked trail, and the fishing trips

(for Russian king crab) that can be arranged at the harbour.
285km (177 miles) northeast of Karasjok, on the border with Russia.

Gjesværstappan

This tiny cliff just off the coast of Magerøya island is home to one of Norway's largest puffin colonies, as well as gannets, eagles, cormorants and other bird life. In summer, regular 'safari' boat trips are organised to the island.

Hammerfest

Another 'northernmost' here, with Hammerfest laying claim to the label of most northerly town in the world, although there are always a few stray contenders to the title. Nevertheless, it's a popular tourist spot, not only as a base point for the surrounding region but for its attractive coastal setting and range of facilities. The town's importance as an Arctic centre is also underlined by the existence of the Royal and Ancient Polar Bear Society, which was established here in the 1960s to protect endangered Arctic animals. Various sculptures, including a polar bear and a ship wedged within pack ice, adorn the town.

Gjenreisningsmuseet (Museum of Postwar Reconstruction)

Finnmark was more or less decimated during World War II, and this is the only museum dedicated to the effort that went into rebuilding the region after the German surrender. The museum examines the cultural and human effect of the war on the local people, and the history and architecture of postwar buildings and accommodation. Attractions include images of north Norway prior to the invasions and replica cave hideouts that locals were forced to take shelter in during the bitter winter in 1944. Another great charm of the museum is its 1950s-style shop.

Kirkegata 21. Tel: (47) 78 40 29 30. www.museumsnett.no/gjenreisningsmuseet. Open: mid-June–mid-Aug Mon–Fri 9am–4pm, Sat & Sun 10am–2pm; mid-Aug–mid-June daily 11am–2pm. Admission charge.

Karasjok

Karasjok is defined by its position as the entrance to Norwegian Lapland,

and influences of its Sami population are everywhere (*see p18*), including a Sami parliament (Sametinget), nature trails incorporating ancient Sami history and an arts centre focusing on traditional crafts. The area also offers numerous opportunities to stay in an authentic Sami camp and discover their fascinating way of life at close hand.

Sámiid Vuorká Dávvirat (Sami Museum)

This open-air environment uncovers various aspects of the Sami culture, from past to present, with Sami buildings gathered together here from various settlements around the region. Of particular interest are the hunting pits for an idea of how Samis traditionally captured wild reindeer.

WORLD WAR II

Despite Norway's attempts to remain neutral during World War II, Germany invaded it in 1940 to prevent a French or British advance, and the nation was thenceforth involved. By 1944, northern Norway had been brought into the fray in a devastating manner because of its location near the Russian border. The Germans applied a scorched earth policy against the region, in an attempt to destroy it before the arrival of the advancing Red Army. Land, warehouses and homes were torched and burned, and many people were left homeless, or fled for their lives to caves in regions such as Bøle, Nordsandfjorden and Kvithellen. Even after the war, many were forced to inhabit caves while new homes and buildings were being built, a situation made even more difficult by the bitterness of the Norwegian winter.

*Museumsgata 17. Tel: (47) 78 46 99 50.
www.karasjokinfo.no. Open: June–mid-
Aug Mon–Fri 9am–6pm, Sat & Sun
10am–6pm; mid-Aug–May Mon–Fri
9am–3pm, Sat & Sun 10am–3pm.
Admission charge.*

Sápmi (Sami Theme Park)

There are more authentic ways of
learning about the Sami culture than
visiting a theme park in their honour,
but this is still an arresting insight into
this deeply traditional way of life in
northern Scandinavia. The intention
here is to inform as well as entertain.
There are reconstructed *siida*
(settlements), complete with reindeer,
handicrafts, costumes, souvenirs to buy
and even Sami food, such as reindeer
broth. The Magic Theatre section is a
state-of-the-art visual and sensory
experience that endeavours to take
visitors back through time to trace the
history of the culture.
*Porsangerveien 1.
Tel: (47) 78 46 88 10.
www.karasjokinfo.no. Open: June–Aug
daily 9am–4pm; Sept–May Mon–Fri
9am–4pm. Admission charge.*

Kautokeino

Reindeer outstrip humans in the large
borough of Kautokeino by 33 to one,
so you can't fail to come across these
gentle creatures during any visit to the
region. Over three-quarters of the
human population here are Samis, and
signs of their colourful culture abound
at every turn. Easter is a particularly

The Nordkapp cliffs are lit by the midnight sun

evocative time to visit the region, when
the Samis hold reindeer races and other
festivals to celebrate the return of the
summer sun.

Guovdageiannu Gilisillju (Sami Settlement Museum)

Probably the country's finest
exploration of the Sami culture, from
its ancient past to its modern-day
rituals. Inside, various farming and
hunting implements and traditional
brightly coloured costumes are on
display, while outside there are
reconstructions of traditional turf huts
in which many Sami still live within
their settlements today.
*Kautokeino. Tel: (47) 78 48 71 00. Open:
mid-June–mid-Aug Mon–Sat 9am–7pm,
Sun noon–7pm; mid-Aug–mid-June
Mon–Fri 9am–3pm. Admission charge.*

Kirkenes

Much of Kirkenes' history is based on
the mining industry, but of far more
interest is its border position with
Russia. Various sights around the town
bear witness to the importance of

Russians here, with a monument commemorating the liberation of the town by the Red Army in 1944, and a Russian market that takes place in the main square on the last Thursday of each month. Kirkenes is also the only official border crossing point between Norway and Russia. Day and weekend trips to Murmansk in Russia can be arranged, providing visas are obtained.

Grenseland Museum

World War II and the mining industry are the main focus of interest in the town's museum. The war section is particularly engaging and details all aspects from the bombing of towns to prison camps and the hardship of life for the local people, including children. The Sami artist John Andreas Savio (1902–38) is honoured here, with displays of his colourful depictions of Sami life and culture on both canvas and woodcuts.

Førstevannslia. Tel: (47) 78 99 48 80.
Open: daily 10am–3.30pm.
Admission charge.

Nordkapp

Not surprisingly, the bleak clifftop landscape of Nordkapp (North Cape), on the island of Magerøya, is one of the most popular spots for tourists to enjoy the midnight sun phenomenon, with the sun sitting doggedly on the horizon all night from May to July.

Nordkappmuseet (North Cape Maritime Museum)

Life on the northernmost tip of the European continent has never been easy, and this intriguing museum explores man's survival in this unforgiving, if striking, environment over the centuries. Among the topics covered are the fishing industry and traditional boat-building.

Pasvik Valley is well known for its flora and fauna

*Fiskeriveien 4, Honningsvåg. Tel: (47) 78
47 72 00. www.nordkappmuseet.no.
Open: June–mid-Aug Mon–Sat
10am–7pm, Sun noon–7pm; mid-
Aug–May Mon–Fri noon–4pm.
Admission charge.*

Pasvikdalen (Pasvik Valley)

Slotted in between the borders of
Russia and Finland, this small slip of
land is renowned for its plant and bird
life, much of which is entirely unique to
the region, and is now preserved in the
national park. Of interest to military
enthusiasts is Vaggetem, where the
remains of a German prisoner-of-war
camp from World War II can still
be seen.

Øvre Pasvik Nasjonalpark
(Pasvik National Park)

Situated in a kind of no-man's-land
between Russia and Finland, this small
park preserves the last primeval forest
in the region and a variety of

indigenous plant species. This is the
largest habitat in Norway for brown
bears and the only place in the
country where they breed. Other
wildlife includes elk, muskrats and
wolverines, while the many bodies of
water are home to pike and perch.
Hiking is popular here too, not least
along the trail that leads to the border
point of all three countries.

Vadsø

During the 17th and 18th centuries,
many Finnish peasants and fishermen
emigrated to Norway, drawn by the
abundance of fish in the waters here. A
large proportion of them settled in and
around Vadsø. Today, peculiarly Finnish
buildings and influences can still be
seen in the region. The wildlife is also
notable here: migratory birds make an
annual stop in the region, and the
ocean is famed for its population of
king crabs.
52km (32 miles) north of Kirkenes by ferry.

Ruija Kvenmuseum (Vadsø Museum)

The town's museum focuses on the
Finnish (Kven) migration and the
language and culture that they brought
with them. Just outside Vadsø town is
the Tuomainengården, where Finnish
businesses, such as a baker and a
blacksmith, as well as a sauna, have
been preserved from the 1850s. The
area is under the Vadsø Museum, with
the same opening times. The museum
also handles the harbour exhibition
focusing on the Amundsen/Nobile

Scenery in Vardø

expedition of 1926 that landed in the town (*see p47*).

Hvistendalsgata 31. Tel: (47) 78 94 28 90. www.museumsnett.no/vadsomuseet. Open: mid-June–mid-Aug Mon–Fri 10am–5pm, Sat & Sun 10am–4pm; mid-Aug–mid-June Mon–Fri 10am–3pm. Admission charge.

Varangerbotn

Nestled within the Varangerfjord region, Varangerbotn is best known for its Sami population, which has been known to have existed here for thousands of years.

Várjjat Sámi Musea (Varanger Sami Museum)

Presented here are all manner of Sami facts and figures, uncovering some of the mysteries and traditions of this ancient northern race (particularly coastal dwelling Sami), and their distinctive art and handicrafts. Of all the Sami centres in the region, this is probably the most modern, utilising audio-visual displays, among other things, to inform visitors. Outside, elements of Sami villages have been reconstructed. The museum also leads guided tours to the Mortensnes site, 20km (12 miles) outside town, where burial and sacrificial sites dating back centuries can still be seen.

Tel: (47) 78 95 99 20. www.varjjat.org. Open: mid-June–mid-Aug daily 10am–6pm; mid-Aug–mid-June Mon–Fri 10am–3pm. Admission charge.

Vardø

Vardø feels like it is perched on the edge of the world, as the most easterly point of Norway and facing the Arctic north. Despite its remote location, the town has been in existence as a trading post since the late 18th century. A century earlier, the town became known as the location of a series of witch hunts, in which some 90 people were accused of consorting with the devil and burned alive. A 'devil's cave' in the 'witch mountain' Domen can still be seen. Not far from Vardø, and worth a visit for its historical value, is Hamningberg. What was once a thriving fishing community has now been abandoned, but its early 20th-century buildings have been preserved as a cultural heritage site.

Vardø museums

The town's museums are a joint enterprise located in two different centres. The **Lushaug** centre has excellent exhibits on the explorers Fridtjof Nansen, who landed here after his bid to reach the North Pole (*see p46*), and Willem Barents, who discovered Svalbard, as well as a detailed description of the 17th-century witch hunts. The **Pomor** museum, set in renovated wharf warehouses, details the Russian trading history of the region.

Tel: (47) 78 98 80 75. www.museumsnett.no/vardomuseene. Open: mid-June–mid-Aug daily 11am–5pm; mid-Aug–mid-June Mon–Fri 4–5pm. Admission charge.

To whale or not to whale?

Man has hunted the world's largest mammal for centuries, as the many prehistoric rock carvings around the world testify, but the first real documentation of Norwegian whaling begins in the Middle Ages. Yet today, of all aspects of Norwegian culture, the issue of whaling is the most controversial and hotly debated.

It was in the early 20th century that concerns were first raised about both the cruelty of the activity and the threat of extinction to the whale community. After World War II, the International Whaling Commission (IWC) was set up, and over the ensuing decades different whale species were gradually withdrawn from the hunting allowances. In 1985, the IWC called for a moratorium on all whaling, unless it is done in the name of scientific research, or, as in the case

The issue of whaling is likely to be debated for many years to come

of the Inuits of Greenland and Alaska, it is seen as part of an ethnic tradition and whale meat is essential for subsistence.

Norway caused much controversy and consternation by objecting to the deal on fairly arbitrary points, and continued to hunt minke whales for commercial purposes from 1993. In addition, in 2004 the parliament announced their intention to increase whaling activities, estimating an annual catch of 1,800 minkes, as opposed to about 160 in 1993. The minke is one of the few whale species that has never been on the endangered list. The country is, however, required to keep the IWC informed on the current count of whales in its waters, and follow strict guidelines, including the type of harpoon used, employing vets to monitor the process, and keeping the hunting within community rather than industrial proportions.

Aside from the IWC, the most vociferous (and, at times, physically threatening) group in the row against Norwegian whaling is Greenpeace, who are generally looked upon with scorn by the northern whalers.

The issue was similar to the British debate about fox hunting, with the

Norwegian whalers considering such environmental groups as urban protestors with no understanding of the rural and coastal way of life. To the outside world, the whalers' actions are seen as barbaric, but for the locals the whalers are highly skilled hunters. The argument is that, without whaling, their communities would be decimated, with the young forced to move south in search of work. Located in the north of the country, the Norwegian whaling industry is conducted between May and August, an annual tradition of livelihood in the area for centuries. Their plea about loss of income usually falls on deaf ears among the protestors, however, as the whaling communities have among the highest per capita income in a country that is known for its high salaries.

Another argument forwarded by the Norwegians is that the greatest threat to the whale population is not whaling but pollution, both through infected water and environmental factors such as unbiodegradable plastic that finds its way into the ocean and chokes the fish on which the whales feed.

There is further international controversy with countries such as Iceland and Japan continuing to whale hunt under the banner of research. But many people, particularly Norwegians, feel this is a falsification, particularly as the whale meat is sold abroad. Japan also claims that it should fall within the traditional sector, like the Inuits, a fact that is disputed by the IWC.

Added to the concerns of whale extinction are the worries of the effects of whaling on other marine life, which would naturally feed off a whale corpse for several months. The other side of this argument is that depletion in whale populations allows for greater fishing opportunities for species such as cod and herring that would otherwise have been food for the whales. The reality, however, is that these fish head towards the shore to escape from the great mammals, making their catch far more straightforward. In Norway, this came to a head as early as 1903 in the village of Mehamn in Finnmark. Fishermen staged a revolt against the whalers, because they felt the culling of whales was diminishing the cod population. The situation became so heated that the army had to be brought in to intervene.

A further complication is that whale-watching as a tourist activity has become a booming industry, particularly in Norway, and that, therefore, the whales have probably as much commercial value to the whaling communities alive as they do dead. Whaling is an issue that looks set to be debated for many years to come.

Svalbard

Situated just south of the North Pole, Svalbard is the remotest region in the Norwegian territory, lying 640km (398 miles) north of the mainland. Svalbard literally means 'cold coast'. Covering an area of 62,050sq km (23,958sq miles), it consists of the islands of Spitsbergen (the largest and only inhabited island), Barentsøya, Prins Karls Forland and several more. Glaciers and icefields cover a large portion of the archipelago, and polar wildlife, including puffins and polar bears, is prolific.

Although some historians believe the Vikings might have discovered the archipelago, its documented history begins in 1596, when the Dutch explorer Willem Barents came across it while in search of the elusive Northeast Passage. The archipelago was incorporated into Norway in 1920. Historically, the islands have been important whaling bases and launching points for explorations to the North Pole, but today they are largely concerned with coal mining and scientific research. Independent travel to Svalbard is rare, with most visitors travelling in organised cruises, but unaccompanied trips are possible provided visitors follow the guidelines set out by the governor of Svalbard (*sysselmann*).

SPITSBERGEN
Adventdalen

Just to the east of Svalbard's capital, Longyearbyen (*see pp144–5*), is the stark landscape of Adventdalen, with hiking or, more safely, driving possibilities (a road sign on the highway warns of polar bear threats). Valley hikes accompanied by husky dogs and trips to an old trappers' station can be arranged.

Barentsburg

Although Svalbard became Norwegian territory in 1920 under the Svalbard Treaty, stipulations ensured that any other nation could also make use of this mineral-rich environment. The one nation that took that to heart was Russia, as a result of which Barentsburg on eastern Spitsbergen is an isolated Russian settlement with about 800 permanent inhabitants, and a Russian consulate. There's even a statue of Lenin here, an image that has long since disappeared from the post-Soviet landscape of the motherland. The sole purpose of the settlement has been coal mining, although this industry is beginning to wane.

Pomor Museum

Barentsburg's only museum unsurprisingly details the history of Russian coal mining in the area, as well as displaying geological exhibits that suggest Russian interest in the region preceded the 16th century.

Ulitsa Ivana Starostina. Open: during cruise visits. Admission charge.

Danskøya

The bleak landscape of Danskøya, a small island off northwest Spitsbergen, is all the more evocative because the remains of various doomed explorations still litter the beach at Virgohamna. The most famous expedition to set off from here was that of three Swedish explorers, led by Salomon August Andrée, who aimed to reach the North Pole in a hot-air balloon in 1897. They were never seen again, but it wasn't until more than 30 years later that the remains of the balloon were found on the island of Kvitøya to the east. Remnants of the team's preparation, including pieces of scrap metal and a ruined cottage, are now protected as a historic monument.

Kongsfjorden

Forming a backdrop to the settlement of Ny-Ålesund (*see p146*) in western Spitsbergen is the beautiful 40km (25-mile)-long Kongsfjorden, with its glacier and diverse geography. The

A walrus taking a nap on one of the small islands in Svalbard

Huskies at Longyearbyen

fjord's particular appeal is its wildlife, which includes seals, polar bears and plentiful bird life. Rising high above it are three gleaming white icecaps.

Krossfjorden

To the south is the surprisingly green area of Krossfjorden, another gem for wildlife lovers. Despite the cold, a number of flower species thrive here, as well as birds and animals including terns, guillemots, Arctic foxes and seals. Graves of whalers dot the region.

Longyearbyen

As the capital of Svalbard, Longyearbyen is visited by most tourists to the region at some point, and for this reason most of the tourist facilities of the archipelago are centred here. That's not to say it's a thriving metropolis; despite its 'capital' tag, only about 1,500 people live here permanently.

Dog sledge trips

One of the most popular activities on Spitsbergen is participating in dog-team sledge trips. Accompanied by experienced guides, you are huddled into ski buggies tied to barking huskies, then whisked through the blinding white landscape to mountain viewpoints and glaciers.

En route the guides point out natural landmarks and the history of the region and its wildlife. Generally trips last about half a day, although there are longer options of several days, overnighting at designated cabins.
Svalbard Villmarkssenter, Longyearbyen. Tel: (47) 79 02 19 85. www.svalbard-adventure.com

Galleri Svalbard

For an insight into the art of the region, a visit to the Galleri Svalbard is a must. Among the exhibits are works by local artists Kåre Tveter and Olaf Storø, images depicting the many exploratory expeditions that have been launched from the region, historic maps, and evocative photographs of the polar sun by Thomas Widerberg. Local handicrafts are also sold here.
PB 475, 9171 Longyearbyen. Tel: (47) 79 02 23 40. Open: Mar–Sept daily 11am–5pm. Free admission.

Graveyard

Overlooking the town from its hilltop site is a slightly macabre but fascinating feature. In 1918, the Spanish flu epidemic raged through Europe, killing millions, but in this remote area, mysteriously only seven men perished. Buried above the town, their graves succumbed to permafrost, potentially freezing the virus in a fossil-like state. Many scientists believe that this could throw light on the epidemic and provide clues to a cure should a similar strain occur again, and research work is being undertaken.

Svalbard Museum

The Svalbard Museum's comprehensive collection traces the history of the entire archipelago. Exhibits detail the discovery of Svalbard, its years as a whaling and trapping region, the expeditions that have been planned and executed from here, the mining industry, and its more troubled role as a battlefield between the British and the Germans during World War II. Also included are elaborate displays examining the flora and fauna of the islands.
PB 521, 9171 Longyearbyen. Tel: (47) 79 02 64 92. www.svalbardmuseum.no. Open: May–Sept 10am–5pm; Oct–Apr noon–5pm. Admission charge.

Magdalenefjord

With its backdrop of pine trees, dazzlingly blue Magdalenefjord, on the northwest coast of Spitsbergen, is probably one of the most beautiful areas of Svalbard and therefore its most popular and touristy. Ideally the thing to do is to sit back and admire the breathtaking scenery around this small fjord, although the tranquillity may be hard to come by if several cruise ships are docking here at once. Historic sights of interest in the area include the graves of 17th- and 18th-century whalers, and the stoves they used to burn whale blubber.

Moffen

The most famous inhabitants of the island of Moffen are the walruses that bask on the shore and breed here between mid-May and mid-September. Because of this, the island has been a protected nature reserve since 1983 and humans are not allowed ashore. However, cruise ships can dock at a certain distance.

Ny-Ålesund

Being able to claim the title of the most northerly permanent settlement in the world might seem an impressive feat: that is, until one realises 'permanent' means around 40 inhabitants. Coal mining was once important here until it was abandoned in the 1960s, and today the town is little more than a research centre. Each summer scientists from all over the world swell the population figures to work on specific projects, but they are a serious lot so they don't add much summer sparkle to the atmosphere. You may have the distinct impression that you are being watched – which you probably are. Tourists have been known on several occasions to disturb scientific instruments and research.

For tourists, the most important sight is the memorial to the explorer Roald Amundsen (*see pp46–7*). In 1926, Amundsen and his friend Umberto Nobile launched their zeppelin *Norge*

POLAR BEARS

Svalbard's most abundant, beautiful but fiercely dangerous inhabitants are its polar bears. These large white mammals (*Ursus maritimus*) roam the icy landscape at will, camouflaged against the snow and protected from the cold by their thick fur and a layer of insulating blubber under their skin. These predatory creatures are the largest land carnivores in the world, with the males averaging 400–600kg (882–1,323lb) in weight. They prey largely on seals, and also walruses, but have no compunction about preying on man whether threatened or not, hence the numerous warnings in Svalbard and the necessity for carrying firearms in unprotected areas. Shooting for game purposes, however, is prohibited as the bears are heavily protected by Norwegian law. Current estimates of the number of polar bears in Svalbard are 2,000, with an individual life expectancy of around 20 years.

from Ny-Ålesund at the start of their successful flight over the North Pole to Alaska. The pylon used for the launch can still be seen and is a protected monument. Sadly, in 1928 Nobile attempted a repeat performance and went missing. Setting out in search of his friend, Amundsen too was never seen again. A bust of this courageous Norwegian now stands in his honour in the town.

UNINHABITED ISLANDS

Unsurprisingly there are numerous uninhabited islands in Svalbard whose size or geography make human habitation unappealing, but they do offer moments of interest for tourists as part of an archipelago cruise.

Bjørnøya does have around ten inhabitants, who staff the meteorological office, but other than that it is protected as a nature reserve. Comprising mountains, lakes and waterfalls, and sandy beaches, it is home to seals and occasional walruses. It is also one of the most striking places to see the midnight sun between May and August. **Kvitøya** was the doomed landing spot for Andrée's balloon flight to the North Pole in the 19th century (*see p143*). Today, it is most appreciated for its pack-ice landscape. Three-quarters of the large island of **Nordaustandlet** are also covered in ice.

Hopen, which also has a few scientist residents, was once known as the prime hunting ground for polar bears until they became protected in the area in 1976; the number of bears has steadily increased since then.

Ny-Ålesund is the most northerly settlement in the world

Getting away from it all

Getting away from it all may seem like a paradoxical phrase in a country whose very essence is geared towards nature and relaxation. Nevertheless, Norway's internationally famed beauty also means crowds, particularly in high summer, and it can sometimes feel like a blow to the senses to combat long queues and clicking cameras amid such serene surroundings. Opting for the lesser known areas other than the classic Oslo to Bergen tourist run will make for a far more enjoyable time if what you are looking for is peace and quiet.

Nature in the city

Oslo and Bergen are vibrant cities on opposite sides of the country but both offer nearby retreats if you are tired of museums and people. From the harbour front in Oslo, ferry trips around the Oslofjord allow a few hours' respite and a chance to see the city's striking surroundings. Also within easy reach of the city are several beaches, including Huk beach on the Bygdøy Peninsula and those on the islands of Hovedøya, Ulvøya and Jeløy.

Bergen is known as the 'gateway to the fjords', so there are plenty of ferry trips available, but instead of heading straight off to the central fjord region, take a boat to the Rjfylke fjord, which attracts far fewer crowds.

In the wilderness

Whether you are seeking pastoral landscapes, pine forests or northern tundra, Norway has a wealth of wilderness areas to dazzle the eyes and clear the mind. In winter, cross-country skiing trails are a wonderful way to immerse yourself in shaded forest areas,

HOLIDAY WITH THE HUSKIES

Huskies may be among the most beautiful canine creatures to outsiders' eyes, but to northern Norwegians they are also an essential pack animal. Before the days of snowmobiles, dog sledges were the only way to reach distant ice-covered valleys for fishing and hunting, and often still are. Various companies offer dog-sledging trips, but one of the best is the **Huskyfarm Innset (Husky Farm)**. Tour guides here explain the history of man's relationship with the huskies, their various uses, and their suitability for the task (namely thick fur and good stamina), before taking visitors out on dog sledge tours through the beautiful mountain landscape. En route visitors are taught how to ride the sledges, chop wood and melt snow for cooking, and look after and interact with the dogs; all in all, a unique and exhilarating experience.

Altevannveien, 9360 Bardu.
Tel: (47) 77 18 45 03. www.huskyfarm.de.
Open: all year round.

while in summer visitors are spoilt for choice by the sheer range of hiking and walking possibilities. You won't be alone on the many marked trails unless you really go off the beaten track, but you can always find a quiet spot to stop for a picnic lunch and just absorb the landscape around you. If you really want to get away from it all, however, head to the north of the country and the remote and windswept region of Finnmark. Traditional Sami settlements, vast snowfields and a bleak but inspiring coastline will make you feel like you are on the edge of the world.

Island-hopping

The Lofoten Islands (*see pp117–23*) are made up of various traditional fishing villages where life still revolves around the annual cod catch and the production of dried cod throughout the year. A holiday spent island-hopping using the various ferries is an unforgettable experience, not just because of the Atlantic landscape of mountains and shores, but also for the glimpses it provides into the fascinating way of life of these hardy villagers. To add to the experience, many companies rent out traditional *rorbuer* (fishermen's huts) to summer tourists (*see p172*)

Getting away from it all

Still waters at Sandøya, southern Norway

Experience the spectacular scenery on a ski-scooter in northern Norway

when the winter fishing season is over. Most are fairly sparsely equipped with beds, a bathroom and a kitchen, but there's no more authentic way to get a sense of life on the edge of the sea. For keen cyclists, touring the islands by bike is also a popular and relaxing activity. The Vesterålen Islands (*see pp124–5*), further north, also offer island-hopping opportunities. Alternatively, take the Hurtigruten ferry route (*see p27*) where you can get on and off wherever you wish between Bergen and Kirkenes.

Svalbard

A visit to the archipelago of Svalbard (*see pp142–7*), lying to the far north of the Norwegian mainland, is the ultimate in 'getting away from it all'.

Offering cruises around the islands are companies such as **Svalbard Polar Travel** (*www.svalbard.polar.com*), which allow visitors an insight into the harsh, isolated conditions of life here, and the chance to see spectacular glacier scenery, as well as walruses and the beautiful but deadly polar bears in their natural habitat.

Water-based holidays

No one should miss the majestic Sognefjord, the largest fjord in the country, but you are unlikely to see it alone if you are visiting Norway in summer. However, most of Norway's fjords have smaller outbranches too narrow for large tourist ferries to explore, and these provide the best opportunities to escape the masses. Renting out a *hytte* (log cabin) often includes the use of a rowing boat moored beside the hut, allowing guests to paddle the gentle waters and find secluded coves and crannies to explore and to swim. If you like messing about on the water in larger boats, head for the Telemark Canal in southern Norway (*see p77*), where you can hire barges to ply up and down the waterway, and negotiate its many locks. Alternatively, book yourself a ride on an organised canal boat; such boats run regularly in summer.

Wildlife watching

Norway has a wealth of wildlife that offers animal lovers quite unique experiences. In the Dovrefjell National Park (*see pp102–3*), safaris can be arranged into the wilderness to spot musk oxen, the distinctive horned bovines whose long-haired coat allows them to adapt to the harsh Nordic climate. The gentle and beautiful reindeer, so beloved of Norwegians, can also be seen here, and you might even spot a brown bear. Moose (elk) safaris can also be arranged.

In the Lofoten Islands and in other parts of the north, whale-watching trips offer the chance to see these magnificent mammals cavorting in the Atlantic waters, a comforting sight for visitors to a country with a controversial whaling history (*see pp140–41*).

Ornithologists will jump at the chance to see the many islands with bird colonies, such as Runde (*see p85*), whose most famous inhabitants are the puffins.

Getting away from it all

Reindeer stroll through the icy Nordic landscape

Shopping

Like everything in Norway, souvenir shopping doesn't come cheap, but the quality lives up to the price tag. Almost all the bigger towns have a wide range of shopping centres and supermarkets, and even the smallest village usually has a crafts store. Museum shops are a good source of souvenirs, particularly the many open-air folk museums, which usually sell variations of traditional crafts, as well as books, tapestries and model houses.

The most popular souvenirs to take home, either as gifts or for yourself, are the traditional brightly coloured knitted sweaters that feature on every tourist brochure. **Dale of Norway**, which can be found in most towns, is the most famous retailer of these items. Jewellery too is of a high standard: Norway has a long tradition of silversmithing, which continues to this day. And even if you don't make it to the far north of the country, Sami costumes and handicrafts are likely to be on sale in most tourist areas.

Smaller, more affordable items are painted woodcarvings, in particular *rosemaling*, and troll figurines. Or why not treat your friends to the pleasure of the Norwegian food that you've enjoyed on holiday, taking home distinctively designed tins of herring and sardines?

OSLO
One of the benefits of shopping in Oslo, particularly in bad weather, is its range of covered malls. **Paléet** (*Karl Johans gate*) is the most elegant, while **Oslo City** (*Stenersgate*) and **Galleri Oslo** (*Vaterland*) offer more standard goods. There are also two large department stores, **GlasMagasinet** and **Steen & Strøm**.

Artisans in the Old Town
In the folk museum (*see p38*) candlemakers, silversmiths and more display their traditional skills and offer their products for sale.
Museumsveien 10.

Bærum Verk
Just outside the city centre is an entire complex devoted to Norwegian crafts, including knitwear, ceramics and wrought-iron pieces. If you have got the time, there's no better place to stock up on souvenirs.
Verksgata 15.

Husfliden
Norwegian national costumes and traditional fishermen's sweaters are the specialities here.
Rosenkrantzgate 8.

Norway Designs

Here, the best buys are the elegantly designed crystal pieces, but other typical souvenirs, such as Norwegian knitwear, ceramics and utensils, are also available.

Stortingsgata 28.

William Schmidt

Within the Paléet shopping mall, this is the best place in the city for Norwegian souvenirs, dolls in national dress, woodcarvings and assorted Viking paraphernalia.

Karl Johans gate 41.

BERGEN

Bryggen and the stalls adjacent to the fish market are the main areas for souvenir shopping. Reindeer skins, which are incredibly warm but light in weight, make for a good buy, as do rugs, traditional knitwear and silver jewellery. The main shopping mall in the centre of the city is **Galleriet**, with more than 70 shops and restaurants. Just south of town is the largest shopping centre in the country, the **Lagunen Storsenter**.

Galleri Bryggen

Various Viking designs can be bought here, in the form of silver jewellery, carvings, ceramics or paintings.

Svensgården-Bryggen.

Julshuset

This year-round Christmas shop sells all types of Christmas decorations, as well as distinctive figures of the Norwegian Santa Claus, known as *Nisse*.

Bryggen 19.

Sesong

The place to go for traditional Norwegian food delicacies.

Vetrildsalmening 2.

Tibords Interiør Bergen Storsenter

If you are looking for traditional ceramics and glassware, this is the place to go to, with many of the goods made by local artisans.

Torgallmenningen 8.

Troll

Any kind of troll figurine or souvenir you can think of can be found in this small waterfront shop.

Bryggen.

Mr and Mrs Claus for sale at the Julshuset in Bergen

Entertainment

Norway's two major cities, Oslo and Bergen, as well as Tromsø in summer, have a vibrant nightlife of bars, clubs and theatres, but outside these urban centres the country is not inclined to party. In summer, various festivals (see pp22–5) keep the action going into the early hours, but high prices restrict most Norwegians (and visitors) from nightly drinking and dancing. Note that since 2004, smoking has been banned in clubs and bars.

Tourist offices

Tourist offices in all the major towns and cities publish an up-to-date *What's On* guide to current events in the area, be it a theatre performance, a festival or a touring rock band gig. This is the easiest and most accurate way to plan your evening's entertainment if you don't feel like hibernating in your hotel bar.

Cinema

Cinema is very popular in Norway. While Norwegian films are screened, the majority of movies are American imports that are screened in English with Norwegian subtitles, making them perfectly accessible to visitors.

OSLO

Oslo's two central cinemas are:
Filmteateret Teletorg
Stortingsgaten 16.
Kinematografer Oslo *Olav V's gate 4.*

BERGEN

The main cinemas in Bergen are:
Konsertpaleet *Neumannsgate 3.*
Forum *Danmarkplass.*

Clubs & bars
OSLO
Bar Babylon

Live DJs and rock music make this a perennially popular venue. There's also outside seating in summer if it all gets a bit loud and sweaty inside.
St Olavs plass 2.

Barbeint

If you are fond of avant-garde and New Wave music then this bar will appeal.
Henrikibsensgate 60A.

Blå

This is the most well-known modern jazz club in the city. Musicians from all over the world come to play here and entertain the mellow crowd.
Brenneriveien 9C.

Bristol Lounge

Recently refurbished, the entertainment complex within the Bristol Hotel offers

two bars and a dance floor. There's also a 'VIP' area for private parties.
Kristian IVs gate 7.

Fridtjof's Pub

Named after the explorer Fridtjof Nansen (*see p46*), this pub has décor commemorating his amazing feats. It is a relaxing, comfy place for a beer and a chat, and in summer there is seating outside.
Fridtjof Nansen's plass 6.

Herr Nilsen

Herr Nilsen is a New-York style jazz bar (minus the cigarette smoke these days, since the smoking ban in 2004) that has live music three nights a week.
C J Hambros plass 5.

Skybar

The top-floor bar of the Radisson SAS Plaza Hotel (*see p174*), Skybar is aptly named. At the top of the tallest building in the country, the views over Oslo as night descends and the city lights up are well worth the price of the drinks.

Radisson SAS Plaza Hotel, Sonia Henies plass 3.

Smuget

Smuget is Oslo's most famous nightclub, with a disco and live performances. There's also a restaurant with an international menu.
Rosenkrantzgate 22.

BERGEN

Altona Vinbar

Altona Vinbar is located in a 17th-century building, but despite the traditional cellar vaults its décor is decidedly minimalist and modern. The atmosphere is equally refined.
Strandgaten 81.

Baklommen

Set in the dark wooded interior of an old Bryggen house, Baklommen is one of the most authentic bars in town.
Bryggen.

The Baklommen bar in Bergen

The entrance to the Konserthus in Oslo

Banco Rotto

Boasting the longest bar in the city, this is an elegant option for a night out – there's a dress code, so no jeans or trainers. Sophisticated, with a more mature clientele.

Vaagsallmenningen.

Christian 49

With an Oriental theme to the décor and cutting-edge music, this is Bergen's most unusual nightclub.

Christian Michelsens gate 4.

Dyvekes Vinkjeller

Part of the charm of the Dyvekes Vinkjeller is that it is said to be haunted by characters from the 17th century, so beware. Other than that, it is a pleasant wine cellar in which to spend an evening.

Hollendergaten 7.

Fincken

Bergen's most popular gay and lesbian venue, where there's always a lively vibe.

Nygårdsgaten 2a.

Kontoret

Next door to the Dickens restaurant (*see p169*), this is one of the liveliest bars in the city.

King Olav V's plass 4.

Mood

With its unique environment and its live performances, Mood is one of Bergen's hottest clubs.

Vågsalmenning 16.

Sørenson Cognac & Sigarbar

As its name suggests, this is a more genteel affair than most, specialising in brandies from around the world and cigars from Cuba and other countries.

C. Sundtsgate 9.

Zachen Piano Bar

Zachen Piano Bar plays live piano music while the clientele can enjoy watching the lights go down over the waterfront. For those who like that sort of thing, there is also karaoke three nights a week.

Torget 2.

Music
OSLO
The National Opera House (Den Norske Opera)

The opera house stages both opera and ballet, by Norwegian as well as touring foreign companies.

Storgata 23.

Oslo Konserthus

The Oslo Konserthus stages regular concerts by the Oslo Philharmonic on Thursdays and Fridays between September and early June.

Munkedamsveien 14.

Oslo Spektrum

The city's main rock concert venue, this regularly features touring international stars such as Rod Stewart.

Sonia Henies plass 2.

Other venues

During the high summer months, the **Norwegian Folk Museum** (*see p38*) is the setting for folk music and dance performances. There are also summer concerts at **Vigeland Park** (*see p42*). One festival in August that will appeal to music lovers is the **Oslo Jazz Festival**.

BERGEN

Bergen Kulturhuset

The Bergen Jazzforum performs both traditional and modern jazz at the Bergen Kulturhuset.

Georgernes Verftsgate 3.

Grieghallen

The Bergen Philharmonic Orchestra and the Bergen Symphony Orchestra both perform concerts in the Grieghallen.

Edvard Grieg's plass 1. Performances Sept–May Thur & Fri night.

Troldhaugen

Concerts are also held at Grieg's former home, Troldhaugen (*see p59*).

Performances mid-June–July.

Theatre
OSLO

Nationaltheater

Ibsen classics are performed regularly (in Norwegian) at the Nationaltheater, but there are also many plays throughout the year (*except mid-June–mid-Aug*) that are performed in English. The tourist office will have details about forthcoming programmes.

Johanne Dybwads plass 1.

BERGEN

Bergen City Theatre

An outdoor play performed here re-creates the city during the 16th century.

Sandviksveien 41. Performances between July & Sept Tue–Sun noon.

Bergen International Theatre

This theatre stages plays in both Norwegian and English.

Nostegaten 54.

Bryggens Museum

Performances of traditional folk dancing are staged at Bryggens Museum (*see p50*).

Performances June & Aug Tue.

Oslo's National Theatre

Children

Norwegians love children, and Norway is an idyllic holiday destination for kids, affording opportunities to roam around safely in the great outdoors and undertake all manner of gentle sporting activities. Furthermore, most hotels will allow a child under 12 to stay for free, and in most museums and sights children under six have free entrance while those under sixteen can enter at half price. Larger restaurants have highchairs for toddlers.

Entry requirements

According to European law, all children must now have their own passport. In addition, single parents may be required to show documentation indicating permission from the absent parent for the child's travel or proving sole parental responsibility. The Norwegian Embassy in your country of residence will be able to offer more information.

Travelling

Distances are vast in Norway, so any holiday with children should be planned sensibly to avoid long road or train journeys. While there is enough to occupy kids in the cities for a couple of days, most children will want to head off to the country as soon as possible. Particularly attractive for children is a stay in a *hytte* (log cabin), many of which include rowing boats in the price (*see p172*).

Beaches

With its long coastline, Norway has no shortage of beach activities. The beaches on the southern coast are especially popular with Norwegian families and therefore have the most child-friendly facilities. In addition, the waters are calm and clean.

Museums

Re-creating the country's landscape of olden times, Norway's abundant open-air museums, such as the Norwegian Folk Museum in Oslo (*see p38*), usually enchant children. By bringing the past to life, they enable kids to engage in history in a very real way. Children will love seeing staff in traditional costumes, wandering cobbled streets and taking part in craft demonstrations.

Norsk Barnemuseum

Kids may groan at the thought of museums, but there is no risk of them getting bored in this one.

Children enjoy the ski slopes

Entirely geared towards children, it has innumerable toys to play with, a treehouse, a haunted attic, painting opportunities and craft workshops.

Sølvberggaten 2, Stavanger. Tel: (47) 51 91 23 93. Open: Tue–Sat 11am–3.30pm, Sun noon–4.30pm. Closed: Mon. Admission charge.

Safaris

Various organisations in the north of the country offer safaris into national parks to see elk and musk oxen, while within the Arctic Circle husky safaris are a complete thrill, with kids also getting to pet and play with the dogs. Tourist offices in the region will have more information on what is on offer during your stay.
www.visitnorway.com

Sports

The fjord region offers some of the best child-friendly outdoor activities in a breathtaking setting that will impress even the youngest eyes. The tranquil fjord waters are ideal for canoeing, and sailing outfits will supply child-sized life jackets. Pony trekking on the gentle

Fjording horses is also a great way to see some of the mountain scenery without tiring out little legs.

Theme parks & funfairs
Bø Sommarland

Norway's largest water park will delight kids of all ages. Among the highlights are a re-created beach, slides, canoes, an artificial wave pool and a 19m (62ft)-high water slope called the Halfpipe. Another major attraction is the Space Ball, a centrifugal ride that spins visitors around in a whirl, then drops them down into a pool. There are also standard funfair rides, arcades and performing acts.

Bø, Skien. Tel: (47) 35 06 16 00.

www.sommerland.no. Open: July–mid-Aug daily 10am–8pm; mid–end June & late Aug Mon–Fri 10am–5pm, Sat & Sun 10am–8pm. Admission charge.

Dyreparken
(Kristiansand Zoo & Amusement Park)

The zoo area in Kristiansand offers children the chance to see many animals indigenous to the country, but they'll probably be more interested in the rides and the water park (*see p64*).

Norgesparken Tusenfryd

The capital's amusement park includes a roller coaster, performing artists and games. There's a daily bus in summer to

Sail on the *Black Lady* pirate ship at the Dyreparken

the park from Oslo's Central Station.
Vinterbro by E6, Oslo.
Tel: (47) 64 97 64 97.
Open: May–Sept daily 10.30am–7pm.
Admission charge.

Vikinglandet

This Viking-themed amusement park is
an animated and entertaining way of
teaching children about Scandinavia's
ancient inhabitants (*see p45*).

The Thunder rollercoaster at Norgesparken Tusenfryd

Sport and leisure

Norwegians adore the great outdoors, and for sports enthusiasts there can be few other countries with greater opportunities to be one with the landscape. In addition, both summer and winter activities are available in equal measure: summer pursuits from May to October and winter sports from around October to February.

Canoeing

What can be more relaxing than softly paddling the calm waters of Norway's many fjords and lakes, taking in the landscape from a canoe? Canoe rental and trips are available all over the country. Voss, in particular, is a prime spot for hiring a sea kayak to explore the tiny inlets and narrow waterways of the fjords (*www.nordicadventures.com*).

Climbing

The most popular climbing and mountaineering areas are the Lofoten Islands, the Lyngen Alps and the fjord region. In summer, mountain and rock

There are no trespassing laws in Norway so walkers can go where they like

Norway is famous for its salmon rivers

climbing are available, while in winter ice climbing on frozen waterfalls and mountain faces offers a challenge to the more experienced. The **Norwegian Mountain Touring Association** (*tel: (47) 22 82 28 00*) can give more information about locations and trips.

Cycling

In southern Norway, in particular, cycling is a great way to see the Sørlandet coast. A popular cycle route is No 3, between Kristiansand and Hovden, which is not only easy-going and suitable for families but covers a great deal of sights and lovely lakelands. Another recommended route is the North Sea Cycle Route in the fjord region. Island-hopping in the north, particularly around the Lofoten Islands, is also an enjoyable experience.

Tourist offices will have details of marked routes as well as information on hiring cycles, or visit the website *www.bike-norway.com*

Fishing

Salmon fishing is a hugely popular sport in Norway, and there are rich salmon rivers all over the country, particularly in the south. The local fishing tax can be paid at tourist information offices, but the state fishing tax must be paid at post offices or online at *www.inatur.no*. A fishing licence is not required to fish in the open sea with a simple rod and line.

Glacier skiing & hiking

There can be few things more exhilarating than skiing in high summer in T-shirts and vests; if you

Horse treks are very popular in Norway

want a spot of winter sports on your summer holiday, Norway's glaciers are the place to visit. Alternatively, there are plenty of organised tours, led by experienced guides, which will allow you to hike on the glacial ice. All equipment is provided on such tours. Contact the Stryn Sommerskisenter (*see p92*) for more information.

Golf

Southern Norway has two 18-hole golf courses, and there are particularly good and attractively set golf courses in Molde and Stavanger, to name just two. Golf has grown in popularity in Norway over recent years, and with the advantage of the midnight sun, which makes play late into the evening possible, one can see why. In addition, Norway doesn't have the strict membership rules of many other countries. Contact the **Norwegian Golf Federation** (*tel: (47) 21 02 91 50*) for more information.

Hiking

Norway has nearly 20,000km (12,427 miles) of hiking trails, making it a major draw for walkers. One of the other great benefits for hikers in Norway is that there are no trespassing laws; the Norwegians' love of the great outdoors means that outlying land is free to all. In general, the season runs from May to October, and the most popular areas are Rondane National Park (*see p107*) or the wilder Dovrefjell (*see pp102–3*), but basically the whole country is a hikers' paradise. The **Norwegian Trekking Association** (*tel: (47) 22 82 28 00*) can give more information about locations and trips.

Horse riding

The Fjording is a breed of horse unique to Norway's fjord region, and various trips and trails are available on horseback in the Nordfjord area, either on organised treks, which are suitable for children, or for those riding independently.

Scuba diving

Norway may not seem an obvious choice for this sport, but the rugged coastline has been the site of many wrecks in the past and various organisations offer guided dives to these time capsules beneath the water. In the Finnmark region, scuba diving to see giant king crabs is also popular.

White-water rafting

Rafting trips vary from the relaxing Class I paddles to the adrenaline-pumping Class V adventures. Among the best areas are Oppdal (*see p107*) and Sjoa (*see pp107–8*).

Winter sports

The winter-sports season usually lasts from October or November to May, depending on snow conditions. Norwegian ski resorts have not attained the international popularity of those in France or Switzerland, largely because of the expense, but nevertheless resorts at places such as Voss and Geilo are superb. Most offer all manner of skiing, from nursery slopes to black runs and off-piste opportunities. Cross-country skiing is also hugely popular, and Norway has numerous marked cross-country trails that are a wonderful way of enjoying the wilderness if you have the stamina. Many of the trails are illuminated at night. Contact **Norske Spor** (*www.skiingnorway.com*) for more information about regions and packages.

Ponds in towns and cities freeze over in winter, turning the summer sunbathing areas into impromptu ice rinks. Many of the larger ones will have areas from where you can hire skates if you feel like gliding about on the ice. In the far north, within the Arctic Circle, snowmobiling training and trips can be arranged for thrilling runs across the ice at high speed (*www.arctictrail.com*).

White-water rafting on the River Oppheimsvatnet near Voss

Food and drink

A wide choice of international cuisine and Norwegian specialities is available in the ever-growing number of eating places across the country. Seafood is abundant, and unusual varieties of meat such as reindeer and elk are on offer. The dampener is the expense: of all things in Norway, the cost of food and drink shocks visitors the most, probably because it is the one aspect that cannot be avoided.

Buying food in supermarkets for picnics in good weather considerably lowers the cost, and if your hotel accommodation includes breakfast, it is wise to make the most of it to stock up for the day. Another budget option (although not the most healthy) is *varm pølse* (hot dogs) which are sold at kiosks, petrol stations and other stalls in towns and cities. Alcohol for personal consumption can only be bought at specially designated shops called *Vinmonopol*, which can be found in most towns.

What to eat

Breakfast
A standard Norwegian *frokost* (breakfast) buffet in hotels will usually consist of various types of bread and crispbreads, eggs, pickled herring, slices of cheese and ham and salad vegetables. Tea might well be served, but coffee is the drink of choice in Norway at any time of the day.

Lunch
The most common *unsj* (lunch) snack is the *smørbrød* (open sandwich) where ham, egg mayonnaise, herring or sardines are the usual toppings.

Cheese and ham are served for breakfast

Dinner

The main meal of the day is the *middag* (evening meal), where you are most likely to find yourself in a restaurant unless you have self-catering accommodation. Fish and seafood dominate the Norwegian menu. Meat is more expensive, but it is worth splashing out at least once to try reindeer. The most common vegetables are potatoes and cabbage.

Specialities

In terms of fish, Norwegian specialities include *tørrfisk* (dried salted cod), *sild* (pickled herring) and *gravlaks* (raw salmon marinated in brandy and dill). Fresh prawns (*reker*) and fish soup (*fiskesuppe*) are also staple menu items. *Lutefisk*, which is another version of dried cod, is served at Christmas time.

Norway produces many cheeses, the most famous internationally being Jarlsberg. Don't miss the chance to try *gudbrandsdalsost*, a type of sweetened goat's cheese. The traditional Norwegian bread is *Lefse*, which is a pancake-style treat cooked on a griddle, but it is less common than it once was. Norwegians tend to prefer more of a crunch to their snacks, so you are most likely to see *flatbrød* (crispbread) everywhere you go.

A speciality pudding, particularly in the north, is *rømmegrøt* (sour cream porridge), while *moltebær* (cloudberries) are a wonderfully unique fruit treat.

Drinks

German-style Pils lager is the most popular drink in Norway, but the national spirit is *aquavit*, which is distilled from potatoes and then flavoured with herbs, most typically caraway, dill and coriander. Wine is available in restaurants and designated shops but is very expensive. Wines that would sell in France or Italy for just a couple of euros, for instance, will easily be charged in double figures in Norway.

The legal drinking age for beer and wine is 18, and for spirits it is 20.

Vegetarians

Unless you are prepared to eat fish or seafood, vegetarian options are fairly limited in Norway and are largely restricted to salads, omelettes and cheese. The larger cities, however, have ethnic restaurants such as Indian and Chinese where vegetarian choices are much more widespread.

COMMON FOOD TERMS

brød bread	**øl** beer
fisk fish	**ost** cheese
grønnsaker vegetables	**poteter** potatoes
is ice ice cream	**ris** rice
kaffe coffee	**sjømat** seafood
kjøtt meat	**smør** butter
kylling chicken	**smørbrød** open
	sandwich
laks salmon	**sukker** sugar
lam lamb	**suppe** soup
melk milk	**te** tea
okse beef	**vanne** water
	vin wine

Where to eat

Most towns and cities in Norway will have a varied selection of pizza and burger restaurants, which are often a lot cheaper than traditional menus, but the list given here concentrates on Norwegian cuisine. The price ratings below are for a three-course meal, without alcohol.

★ Less than 200 Nkr
★★ 200–400 Nkr
★★★ 400–600 Nkr
★★★★ Over 600 Nkr

OSLO

Det Gamle Rådhus ★★
Built in 1641, Oslo's first Town Hall is now the setting for an elegant restaurant, with fish as the main speciality. Visitors during the Christmas period shouldn't miss the acclaimed *lutefisk* spread.
Nedre Slottsgate 1, Christiania Torg.
Tel: (47) 22 42 01 07.
Closed: Sun.

D/S Louise Restaurant & Bar ★★
With its lovely harbour setting and range of maritime memorabilia, this is one of Oslo's most popular restaurants, serving both Norwegian and international menus. The lunchtime *smørbrød* buffet is good value.
Stranden 3.
Tel: (47) 22 83 00 60.

Engebret Café ★★
Housed in an 18th-century building, Oslo's oldest restaurant specialises in Norwegian cuisine, including seafood and game. The sandwich buffet at lunchtime is a good budget option, and there is outdoor seating during the summer.
Bankplassen 1.
Tel: (47) 22 82 25 25.

Det Gamle Rådhus is located in Oslo's old Town Hall

Grand Café ★

Oslo's most famous café, located within the Grand Hotel (*see p174*), also serves full meals, such as reindeer steaks, based on very traditional Norwegian cuisine.

Karl Johans gate 31.
Tel: (47) 23 21 20 00.

Kaffistova ★★

Opened at the turn of the 20th century, this lovely café serves delicious local specialities such as meatballs, potato dumplings and sour cream porridge. It benefits from its central location, making an ideal lunch spot while sightseeing along Karl Johans gate.

Rosenkrantzgate 8.
Tel: (47) 23 21 41 00.

Oro ★★★★

Winner of a Michelin star in 2004, there is a range of dining options here, from the high-class restaurant offering a tasty menu of lobster and foie gras, among other things, to the more relaxed tapas-style bar. There's also a shop selling Norwegian delicacies.

Tordenskioldsgate 6A.
Tel: (47) 23 01 02 40.

Solsiden Restaurant ★★★

Lovers of seafood should make a beeline for Solsiden, where oysters, monkfish, salmon and tanks of live lobsters are the speciality. In addition, its location on the harbour offers wonderful views well into the late summer evening.

Søndre Akershus Kai 34.
Tel: (47) 22 33 36 30.
Closed: Oct–Apr.

Statholdergaarden ★★★★

Food critics continually rave about the freshest of fresh Norwegian cuisine served here, which is enhanced by a modern twist, but you certainly pay for the privilege. Leave room for the cloudberry pancakes for dessert.

Rådhusgate 11.
Tel: (47) 22 41 88 00.

BERGEN

Bryggeloftet & Stuene ★★

Two restaurants in one, with the downstairs serving snacks, while the restaurant upstairs serves fish specialities such as salmon and herring. This is possibly the most traditional place in the city, and it won't break the bank.

Bryggen 11–13.
Tel: (47) 55 30 20 70.

Dickens ★

With its central location and old-fashioned décor including a zinc bar counter, this is a popular lunch spot for locals.

Kong Olav V's plass 4.
Tel: (47) 55 36 31 30.

Enhjørningen ★★★

Set in a former merchant's warehouse full of antiques, Enhjørningen is a great fish restaurant on the waterfront. Try the angler fish or the mussel soup.

Bryggen.
Tel: (47) 55 32 79 19.

Finnegårdstuene ★★★

In this converted old warehouse, French and Norwegian cuisine are

combined innovatively. The menu changes with the season to ensure the inclusion of fresh ingredients.
Rosenkrantzgaten 6.
Tel: (47) 55 55 03 00.

Fløien Folkerestaurant ★★

Take the funicular up to Mount Fløien (*see pp55–6*) and enjoy a traditional dinner with wonderful views down over the harbour.
Fløyfjellett 2.
Tel: (47) 55 33 69 99.

Nad's Dining Experience ★★★

This new restaurant has been given the title 'the best seafood place in Bergen', and the fish tanks here prove just how fresh the food is. Plus, there are great views of the harbour.
Zachariasbrygge 50.
Tel: (47) 55 55 96 46.

Potetkjelleren ★★★

A wonderfully romantic venue set in vaulted whitewashed cellars. As usual, the emphasis is on fish, and there's an extensive wine list too.

Kong Oscars gata 1.
Tel: (47) 55 32 00 70.

OTHER TOWNS AND AREAS
Ålesund
Hummer og Kanari ★★

Decorated with photographs of Ålesund (*see pp82–3*), before and after its tragic fire, this is certainly the best restaurant in town, with wonderful fish dishes.
Kongens Gate 19.
Tel: (47) 70 12 80 08.

Karasjok
Nedre Mollisjok Fjellstue ★★

In this remote mountain lodge, traditional Sami recipes are prepared with care. Trout, Arctic char and perch are often on the menu, fresh from the river, as well as grouse and cloudberries.
Mollisjok.
Tel: (47) 78 44 76 00.

Kristiansand
Sjøhuset ★★

There are numerous restaurants along the town's waterfront but this is one of the finest, with a wide range

of fresh seafood on offer.
Østre Strangate 13.
Tel: (47) 38 02 62 60.

Lillehammer
Vertshuset Solveig ★

Set in the oldest building in town, this bustling place serves Norwegian classics such as trout and reindeer.
Storgata 68B.
Tel: (47) 61 26 27 87.

Lofoten Islands
Fiskekrogen, Henningsvaer ★★★

Set in the port's former fish factory, seasonal fish is the order of the day, especially the speciality, cod. There's also caviar home-made by the chef. If you can't decide between the many options, go for the seafood platter to sample all that's best.
Dreyersgate 19.
Tel: (47) 76 07 46 52.

Stavanger
Sjøhuset Skagen ★

Traditional Norwegian cuisine is served in one of Stavanger's old buildings, filled

At Bergen Food Hall by the harbour, you can buy locally produced cheese and high-quality meat, including salted and cured sheep's head

with small cubicles and offering a distinctly historic atmosphere.
Skagenkaien 16.
Tel: (47) 51 89 51 80.

Tromsø

Arctandria ★★
In a warehouse setting, fish is once again on the menu in this northern coastal town, but there's also whale and seal meat for those with an unenvironmental appetite. Better to go for the traditional stockfish (dried cod).

Strandtorget 1.
Tel: (47) 77 60 07 20.

Emma's Drømmekjøkken ★★★
Possibly one of the most renowned restaurants in northern Norway, this has a menu focusing on specialities of the northern regions, including Arctic char and oysters.
Kirkegata 8.
Tel: (47) 77 63 77 30.

Trondheim

Grenaderen ★★
In this candlelit 19th-century building, try the pickled elk then the cloudberry ice cream.
Kongsgårdsgata 1.
Tel: (47) 73 51 66 80.

Vadsø

Havhesten ★★
This restaurant, located just out of town, serves the best seafood and meat dishes in the area. Don't miss the fish soup. It's only open in the summer months.
Ekkerøy.
Tel: (47) 90 50 60 80.

Hotels and accommodation

The standard of accommodation in Norway is extremely high, and even at the lowest end of the market you are likely to find immaculately clean rooms and hot running water. The big cities have plenty of high-end chain hotels with luxury facilities, while in smaller towns and villages family-run guesthouses and rented fishermen's huts offer an unbeatable experience.

Hotels

In all the major cities, you will find the Norwegian chain hotels of Rainbow, Rica and Radisson SAS, all of which offer very sophisticated facilities. Cheaper chains include the Best Western and Comfort Inn hotels.

Guesthouses & apartments

Throughout the country, there are guesthouses and pensions that are usually family-run with only a small number of rooms, but they make for a more personal stay than large hotels and are considerably cheaper. In cities such as Bergen and Oslo, particularly during the summer months, there is a range of apartments to rent, which are usually studio-type rooms (often occupied by university students during the academic year) with beds and a small kitchenette.

Cabins

All along the coast, but predominantly in the Lofoten Islands, *rorbuer* (traditional fishermen's cabins) can be rented for holiday stays, making for a memorable experience. A boat is often included in the rate. There are also plenty of *hytte* (log cabins), which offer cosy accommodation, and in Finnmark in the north there are numerous mountain lodges run by Samis, who prepare traditional dishes and organise cultural tours (*www.samitour.no*).

Hytte are cosy log cabins

DNT mountain huts

The DNT (Den Norske Turistforening) organisation maintains more than 400 huts along mountain hiking trails, arranged so that they are no more than a day's hike apart. They are an invaluable resource for those walkers who want to spend a considerable part of their holiday on an uninterrupted hike. All the huts have beds and cooking facilities, but some are staffed, and some not. For the latter, it is necessary to arrange for key collection from a DNT office in advance. Lodgings cannot always be booked in advance: however, DNT say that everyone who comes to a cabin will have a place to sleep, even if this is a mattress on the floor. Most huts are closed between October and February.

Hostels

Vandrerhjem (youth hostels) offer dormitory-style accommodation and communal cooking facilities. Despite their name, there is no age barrier for staying in one, and they are a good option for those on a budget.

Camping

Campsites are given different star ratings, much the same as hotels, depending on the facilities they provide. Most offer pitching sites for tents, hook-ups for RV camper vans and, in some cases, small cabins equipped with bunk beds and kitchenettes. Note that no open fires are permitted during summer, and that most campsites close during the winter months.

The campsite at Oppdal blends in with the landscape

Where to stay

The following list of accommodation shows price ranges that will help you select an appropriate place:

★   Less than 500 Nkr
★★   500–1,000 Nkr
★★★   1,000–1,500 Nkr
★★★★   Over 1,500 Nkr

OSLO

Comfort Hotel Gabelhus ★★★

Built in 1912, this has always been a popular place to stay in the city, and after an expansion in 2004 it can now accommodate even more guests. Antique furniture and open fireplaces add to the traditional atmosphere of the hotel.
Gabels Gate 16.
Tel: (47) 23 27 65 00.

First Hotel Millennium ★★

A good-value central base in the city, flaunting a mixture of contemporary design and art deco. The top-floor rooms benefit from balconies.
Tollbugaten 25.
Tel: (47) 21 02 28 00.

Grand Hotel ★★★

The best-known hotel in the city and probably the country, this bastion of elegance is still going strong. The rooms are elegantly furnished, and the en-suite facilities are stylishly done in marble. The hotel's café (*see p169*) was a regular haunt of Ibsen and Munch.
Karl Johans gate 31.
Tel: (47) 23 21 20 00.

Hotel Bastion ★★★

This new boutique hotel has been elegantly designed by Anemone Våge. Rooms are stylish, and some of the bathrooms feature Jacuzzis. The bar in the foyer is a popular meeting place for well-heeled Oslovians.
Skippergaten 7.
Tel: (47) 22 47 77 00.

The Grand Hotel in Oslo

Hotel Bristol ★★★★

Opulence reigns supreme here, with the grand foyer decorated with chandeliers and pillars dating from the 1920s, and rooms done up lavishly. The atmosphere of the hotel, however, is refreshingly informal.
Kristian IV's gate 7.
Tel: (47) 22 82 60 00.

Radisson SAS Plaza Hotel ★★★★

The tallest building in Norway, the Plaza's rooftop bar offers the best view to be had of the city. The rooms are designed in a contemporary style, and the restaurant serves innovative dishes based on traditional Norwegian cuisine.
Sonia Henies plass 3.
Tel: (47) 22 05 80 10.

BERGEN

Crowded House Travel Lodge ★

Plain and simple, this is the best value in central Bergen, but don't expect any mod-cons. It is predominantly popular with students and those trying their best to see Norway on a budget.

Håkonsgaten 27.
Tel: (47) 55 90 72 00.

Hanseatic Hotel ★★

Opened in 2006 right in the Bryggen district of the city, this lovely boutique-style hotel has 16 rooms and has preserved its historic interior of wooden beams and traditional furniture. Good value in such a central district.
Rosenkrantzgaten 6.
Tel: (47) 53 30 48 00.

Marken Gjestehus ★

This centrally located guesthouse has a range of single rooms and dormitory-style accommodation, offering great value for money. There is also a communal living room, kitchen and laundry.
Kong Oscarsgate 45.
Tel: (47) 55 31 44 04.

Radisson SAS Royal Hotel ★★★★

One of the best hotels in the city, both for its location and its amenities. Its pub is very popular in summer.
Bryggen.
Tel: (47) 55 57 30 30.

Steens Hotel ★★

Set in a former 19th-century private home,

the hotel has 20 rooms that are all elegantly furnished and equipped with Internet facilities.
Parkveien 22.
Tel: (47) 55 30 88 88.

Strand Hotel ★★

With wonderful views of the Bryggen and the Fish Market, this is one of the prime hotels in the city. There is an elegant bar area, a roof terrace in summer and a fitness centre. All rooms have Internet facilities.
Standkaien 2–4.
Tel: (47) 55 59 33 00.

OTHER TOWNS AND AREAS
Ålesund

Comfort Hotel Bryggen ★★

As its name suggests, this is a wonderfully comfortable and cosy hotel, set in a gabled building with open fires and antiques on display. Some rooms have waterfront views.
Apotekergata 1–3.
Tel: (47) 70 12 64 00.

Bodø

Rica Hotel Bodø ★★

Simple, clean and modern, this makes

for a good-value option if you are staying overnight in Bodø.
Sjøgata 23.
Tel: (47) 75 54 70 00.

Flåm

Fretheim Hotel ★★★

This distinctive hotel overlooking the waterfront at Flåm is renowned for its architecture, cleverly combining the original 1870 building with a modern glass-fronted extension. The restaurant is the best in town.
Tel: (47) 57 63 63 00.

Geiranger

Hotell Geiranger ★★★

Some rooms here have balconies looking directly out on to the fjord, and there's an excellent restaurant in which you can either opt for the à la carte menu or enjoy the traditional buffet.
Tel: (47) 70 26 30 05.

Union Hotel ★★★

Built in 1891, this is a perennially popular small hotel in the region, with opulent furnishings and an excellent traditional restaurant.
Tel: (47) 70 26 83 00.

Haugesund

Radisson SAS Park Hotel ★★★

Beautifully situated and benefiting from a pool, this is one of the nicest places to stay in the area, with the style and facilities associated with the Radisson chain.
Ystadveien 1.
Tel: (47) 52 86 10 10.

Karasjok

Engholm's Huskyi Lodge ★

It does not get more authentic than this selection of log cabins with kitchenette facilities, just outside town. Even more entrancing are the many tours arranged from here, including dog sledging. A communal cabin with an open fire is the setting for evening social activities.
Tel: (47) 78 46 71 66.

Rica Hotel Karasjok ★★

With forest views and a lively atmosphere, this is certainly the best option within the town centre. Rooms are contemporary in design, and the staff are extremely helpful.

Porsangerveien 1.
Tel: (47) 78 46 74 00.

Kristiansand

Clarion Hotel Ernst ★★★

Probably the most popular place to stay in a town that is rather lacking in good accommodation. Although elements of its 19th-century history have been retained in the décor, overall this is a modern, efficient option for a comfortable stay.
Rådhusgaten 2.
Tel: (47) 38 13 86 00.

Lærdal

Lindstrøm Hotel ★★

This lovely hotel is situated right in the heart of Lærdalsøyri, the old quarter of town with its pastel-painted wooden houses. All the rooms have mountain views. The restaurant serves a traditional buffet in the evening, and there is live piano music in the bar.
Tel: (47) 57 66 69 00.
Closed: Oct–Apr.

Lillehammer

First Hotel Breiseth ★★★

Pillars, open fires and wooden décor are all features of this centrally located hotel, which has been in operation since the turn of the 20th century.
1–5 Jembanegaten 1.
Tel: (47) 61 24 77 77.

Lofoten Islands

Svinøya Rorbuer, Svolvær ★★

No trip to the Lofotens would be complete without a stay in a traditional *rorbu* (fisherman's hut), and here there is a cluster of them, operated from a central reception area. All have bathrooms and cooking facilities.
Gunnar Bergs vei 2.
Tel: (47) 76 06 99 30.
www.svinoya.no

Molde

Rainbow Hotel Moldefjord ★★

Between the mountains and the shore, this chain hotel is one of the nicest and best-value places to stay in town.
Storgate 8.
Tel: (47) 71 20 35 00.

Mosjøen

Norlandia Lyngengården Hotell ★★

A convenient if slightly impersonal place to stay, this chain hotel has all modern facilities and is located near the Vefsnfjord, noted for its salmon fishing.
Vollanveien 15.
Tel: (47) 75 17 48 00.

Nordkapp

Repvåg Fjord Hotell and Rorbuer ★★

With 70 comfortable rooms, this large coastal hotel is renowned in the region for its excellent seafood restaurant. There is also a sauna and a fitness centre.
Tel: (47) 78 47 54 40.

Sæbø

Hotell Sagafjord ★★★

With one of the most attractive settings of any hotel in Norway, the Sagafjord is ideally located for visiting the Geiranger and Briksdalsbreen glaciers. The restaurant is highly rated, and there is a children's playground with goats to play with.
Sæbø 6165.
Tel: (47) 70 04 02 60.

Stavanger

Skagen Brygge Hotell ★★★

At the heart of this hotel, right on the waterfront, is an original 19th-century building; the modern structure around it has been built imitating the older design. With wooden floors and high windows, rooms vary between traditional chintz and modern contemporary design.
Skagenkeien 30.
Tel: (47) 51 85 00 00.

Tromsø

Scandic Hotel Tromsø ★★★

This chain hotel has its own nightclub, which is a popular gathering place for locals in the lively town of Tromsø. Other amenities include a pool, sauna and solarium.
Helloveien 23.
Tel: (47) 77 75 50 00.

Tromsø Vandrerhjem ★

For those on a budget, this youth hostel is a good option.
Åsgårdveien 9.
Tel: (47) 77 65 76 28.
Open: June–Aug.

Trondheim

Clarion Collection Hotel Grand Olav ★★★

Without a doubt the most stylish hotel in town, and with the added benefit of a central location.
Kjøpmannsgata 48.
Tel: (47) 73 80 80 80.

Vadsø

Rica Hotel Vadsø ★★★

This elegant but modern hotel is part of the Norwegian Rica hotel chain. All rooms are fully equipped, and there is a good restaurant.
Oscarsgate 4.
Tel: (47) 78 95 52 50.

Voss

Fleischer's Hotel ★★

Right next to the railway station and with lovely lakeside views, this is the landmark hotel in Voss. Rooms are modern and comfortable, and a lot of effort has been put in to cater to children's needs.
Evangervegen.
Tel: (47) 56 52 05 00.

Practical guide

Arriving

Citizens of countries other than those within the Schengen region need a valid passport to enter Norway. For visitors from some countries, a visa is also required. Contact the Norwegian Embassy or Consulate in your country for further information.

By air

Oslo's international airport, Gardermoen, is serviced by numerous airlines including SAS (Scandinavian Airlines), British Airways and Icelandair. The budget airline Ryanair also flies from London to Torp, an airport about 100km (62 miles) south of Oslo, and to Haugesand. Kristiansand, Bergen, Trondheim, Stavanger and Tromsø also have international airports.

By bus

The Norway Bussekepress companies run regular express routes between Stockholm, Gothenburg and Malmö in Sweden and Oslo, and there is also the option of continuing from Sweden to Berlin in Germany. In the north, there is a daily bus in summer between Rovaniemi in Finland and Tromsø.

By car

Motorways run between Stockholm and Gothenburg and Oslo, and border crossings are straightforward: you may not even have to show your passport although you should have it handy. A car ferry operates between Denmark and Kristiansand.

By sea

DFDS (*tel: (47) 66 81 66 00*) operates a ferry service between Newcastle in the UK and Gothenburg in Sweden to Kristiansand. **Color Line** (*tel: (47) 22 94 44 00*) also has a regular ferry service between Hirtshals in Denmark and Kristiansand or Bergen. **Fjord Line**'s (*tel: (47) 55 32 37 70*) ferry service is between Newcastle and Bergen.

By train

There is a daily train service between Stockholm and Oslo, Trondheim and Narvik. There is also a train between Copenhagen and Oslo, which boards a special ferry for the short sea crossing. For up-to-date details of rail services, consult the *Thomas Cook European Rail Timetable*, which is published monthly (*see p184–5*).

Climate

The best time to visit Norway is between May and August, when the weather is considerably warmer, but a warm fleece or jacket as well as an umbrella should always be part of your luggage.

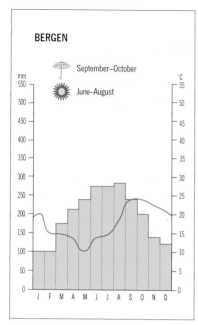

BERGEN

September–October

June–August

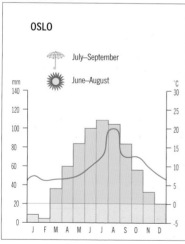

OSLO

July–September

June–August

**WEATHER CONVERSION
CHART**

25.4mm = 1 inch

°F = 1.8 × °C + 32

Practical guide

Crime & safety

Norway is probably one of the safest countries in the world in terms of crime, but to be on the safe side, leave valuables in the hotel safe and out of sight when leaving a parked car. Pickpockets do operate in Oslo, particularly around the central station, so keep an eye on your belongings.

Customs regulations

Alcohol imports are limited to 2 litres (4pts) of beer, 1 litre (2pts) of spirits and 1 litre (2pts) of wine. Visitors may also import 200 cigarettes and gifts valued at 1,200 Nkr or below.

Driving
Car hire

All the major car hire firms such as Avis, Budget, Hertz and Europcar have offices in Norway's international and domestic airports and in major cities. Car hire, however, is very expensive, so it might be worth making use of the far cheaper weekend deals, hiring a vehicle from Friday afternoon until Monday morning.

Emergency

For breakdown assistance, telephone *8100 0505* or, if you are a member of an automobile association in your own country, you can get affiliated assistance from the **Norges Automobil Forbund** (*tel: (47) 22 34 16 00*). Emergency telephones can be found along motorways.

Practical guide

Insurance

Third-party insurance is compulsory in Norway, and a Green Card is also recommended.

Petrol

Petrol is available in leaded and unleaded form, and petrol stations in cities and larger towns are usually open until at least 10pm, while some offer 24-hour service. In smaller, more rural regions, however, it is essential to check opening times, as many petrol stations close as early as 6pm and sometimes for the entire weekend. Diesel is almost essential in winter because it does not freeze.

Roads

Norwegians drive on the right side of the road. The large majority of road signs in Norway use international highway code symbols. There are a great number of toll roads in Norway, and most of them are automated by the

A Father Christmas road sign in Akerhaus

SAFETY IN SVALBARD

The risks involved for unprepared tourists in Svalbard cannot be overestimated. Ice packs and glaciers are death-traps to the uninitiated, and visits should always be undertaken with a guide or with a group connected via a safety rope, and crampons worn on boots. In summer, the rivers too are dangerous places because of the icy swell brought about by melting snow. The very real risk to anyone visiting Svalbard, however, is the polar bears, which can be encountered just about anywhere; they are often seen rummaging through wastebins in Longyearbyen (*see pp144–5*) itself. For those with weapon training, carrying a rifle is recommended; those without training should never leave populated areas without a qualified guide. A signal pistol is also advisable for scaring away the bears, who are notoriously short-sighted. Warning flares should also be set up at campsites.

AutoPASS subscription system. The easiest way for tourists to pay is either at petrol stations, or to await an invoice that is mailed to them, based on the licence registration number. It is obligatory to drive with dipped headlights, and to wear both front and rear seat belts. Children under four should be seated in a special baby seat. If driving in snowy conditions, tyre chains should be attached to the wheels.

Speed limits

The speed limit in towns and cities is 50km/h (31mph), on open roads 80km/h (50mph), and on motorways 90km/h (56mph). Limits are strictly enforced in Norway, and speeding fines are very high.

Keep tyre chains on during the winter snow

Electricity

Norway uses 220 volts and two-pin European plugs.

Embassies & consulates

Australia

Jernbanetorget 2, Oslo.
Tel: (47) 22 47 91 70.

Canada

Bergen: *Asbjørnsensgate 20.*
Tel: (47) 55 29 71 30.
Oslo: *Wergelandsveien 7.*
Tel: (47) 22 46 69 55.

Ireland

Drammensveien 126A, Oslo.
Tel: (47) 22 12 20 00.

United Kingdom

Bergen: *Øvre Ole Bulls Plass 1.*
Tel: (47) 55 36 78 10.
Oslo: *Thomas Heftyes gate 8.*
Tel: (47) 23 13 27 00.

United States of America

Drammensveien 18, Oslo.
Tel: (47) 22 44 85 80.

Emergency telephone numbers

Police *112*
Fire *110*
Ambulance *113*

CONVERSION TABLE

FROM	TO	MULTIPLY BY
Inches	Centimetres	2.54
Feet	Metres	0.3048
Yards	Metres	0.9144
Miles	Kilometres	1.6090
Acres	Hectares	0.4047
Gallons	Litres	4.5460
Ounces	Grams	28.35
Pounds	Grams	453.6
Pounds	Kilograms	0.4536
Tons	Tonnes	1.0160

To convert back, for example from centimetres to inches, divide by the number in the third column.

MEN'S SUITS

UK	36	38	40	42	44	46	48
Rest of Europe	46	48	50	52	54	56	58
USA	36	38	40	42	44	46	48

DRESS SIZES

UK	8	10	12	14	16	18
France	36	38	40	42	44	46
Italy	38	40	42	44	46	48
Rest of Europe	34	36	38	40	42	44
USA	6	8	10	12	14	16

MEN'S SHIRTS

UK	14	14.5	15	15.5	16	16.5	17
Rest of Europe	36	37	38	39/40	41	42	43
USA	14	14.5	15	15.5	16	16.5	17

MEN'S SHOES

UK	7	7.5	8.5	9.5	10.5	11
Rest of Europe	41	42	43	44	45	46
USA	8	8.5	9.5	10.5	11.5	12

WOMEN'S SHOES

UK	4.5	5	5.5	6	6.5	7
Rest of Europe	38	38	39	39	40	41
USA	6	6.5	7	7.5	8	8.5

Practical guide

Health & insurance

There are no vaccinations required to visit Norway, although inoculation against tetanus is always advisable. Tap water is safe to drink all over the country. All doctors, hospital staff and pharmacists have a good command of English. Health care is free for European citizens, provided they are carrying a European Health Insurance Card (available online at *www.ehic.org.uk*; *tel: 0845 606 2030* or from post offices in the UK). For minor ailments, *apotek* (pharmacists), indicated by a green cross above their door, can be found in all towns and cities. If travelling to the north in summer take a good insect repellent, as midges and non-malarial mosquitoes are a major nuisance. If you are bitten badly, a pharmacist will be able to supply a non-prescriptive antihistamine cream. Note that some medicines, such as codeine, which are easily available over the counter in other countries, require a prescription in Norway.

Internet

Internet facilities are easy to come by in Oslo and Bergen, but elsewhere you may find only one or two places with Internet access, usually libraries, and therefore long queues. You will need to put your name on a list to get half an hour of allotted time. Most high-range hotels now include Internet facilities, either in individual rooms or in public areas near the reception.

Media

In large cities such as Oslo and Bergen, the major British newspapers can usually be found, but may be a day after publication. Magazines such as *Time* and *The Economist* are also available, as is the *International Herald Tribune*. The leading Norwegian papers are *Aftenposten* and *Bergens Tidende*. The *Norway Post* is an online newspaper in English (*www.norwaypost.no*). The Norwegian broadcasting network NRK predominantly broadcasts in Norwegian, but British and American imports are presented in their original language with Norwegian subtitles. Most high-end hotels have cable TV with English channels.

Money matters

Currency

The currency is the Norwegian krone (NOK or Nkr), and one Nkr is made up of 100 øre. Coins come in the following denominations: 50 øre and 1, 5, 10 and 20 Nkr. Nkr notes come in 50, 100, 200, 500 and 1,000 denominations.

Credit cards

All the major credit cards – Visa, MasterCard, American Express and Diners Club – are readily accepted across Norway, except perhaps in the smallest shops.

Exchange

Most major towns and cities have automated teller machines (known as

Language

Despite having two official languages, the majority of people speak Bokmål. There are 29 letters in the Norwegian alphabet, which includes all the letters of the Latin alphabet as well as æ, å and ø.

PRONUNCIATION

æ	as the e in 'bed'
å	as the o in 'sword'
ø	as the e in 'her'
ai	as in 'eye'
ei	as in 'bay'
h	silent before v and j
j	as the y in 'year'
rs	as the 'sh' in 'wish'
v	as the w in 'wear'

GREETINGS & POLITENESS

Hello	Goddag
Goodbye	Morna
Good morning	God morgen
Good evening	God aften
Good night	God natt
Please	Vær så snill
Thank you	Takk
Excuse me	Unnskyld

NUMBERS

1	en	**8**	åtte
2	to	**9**	ni
3	tre	**10**	ti
4	fire	**20**	tjue/tyve
5	fem	**100**	hundre
6	seks	**1,000**	itusen
7	sju		

DAYS OF THE WEEK

Monday	Mandag
Tuesday	Tirsdag
Wednesday	Onsdag
Thursday	Torsdag
Friday	Fredag
Saturday	Lørdag
Sunday	Søndag

EVERYDAY EXPRESSIONS

Yes	Ja
No	Nei
There is	Det er
There is not	Det er ikke
I want	Jeg vil ha
How much?	Hvor mye koster det?
Expensive	Dyr
Cheap	Billig
Money	Penger
Toilet	Toalett
Men's toilet	Menn toalett
Women's toilet	Kvinner toalett
Time	Tid
Today	i dag
Yesterday	i går
Tomorrow	i morgen
What is the time?	Hva er klokka?

'mini banks') that accept certain foreign credit and debit cards. Traveller's cheques in major currencies can be exchanged in banks and post offices.

National holidays

1 January New Year's Day
March–April
Easter Friday–Easter Monday
1 May Labour Day
17 May National Constitution Day
25 December Christmas Day
26 December Boxing Day

Opening hours

Shops are usually open Monday–Wednesday and Friday from 9am–5pm, Thursday until 7pm and Saturday until 3pm. Most banks are open Monday–Friday from 9am–3.30pm (Thursday until 5.30pm). Supermarkets and shopping centres, particularly in the larger cities, usually stay open until 8pm.

Organised tours

Tourist offices all over the country will be happy to organise specialised tours for you, be it a whale-watching trip, a marked hike or a city tour. One of the most popular tours is the 'Norway in a Nutshell' tour (*www.fjordtours.no*), which can be arranged at tourist offices and railway stations. The most common tour under this banner is from Oslo to Bergen, taking in the fjords and the Flåm railway en route, but be aware

that its popularity means it is very crowded.

Pharmacies

Pharmacies are open during business hours, and pharmacists are highly qualified in diagnosing and treating minor ailments, as well as being fluent in English. If you need a pharmacist outside business hours, there will be a sign in the window indicating the nearest all-night pharmacy.

Police

The Norwegian police service is divided into 27 districts, but they all come under the jurisdiction of the National Police Service. They can be identified by the royal coat of arms on their uniforms and should be consulted immediately if you are a victim of crime of any sort.

Post offices

Norway has *poster kontor* (post offices) in all towns and cities, and they are open Monday–Friday 8.30am–4pm and Saturday 8am–1pm. Poste restante services are available. Wall-mounted postboxes are bright red and decorated with a trumpet symbol. Stamps can be bought at post offices as well as at newspaper stands and anywhere that you can buy postcards.

Public transport
Thomas Cook Timetable

For details and times of train, ferry and long-distance bus services consult the *Thomas Cook European Rail Timetable*, (published monthly), which can be bought online at *www.thomascookpublishing.com*, from branches of Thomas Cook in the UK or by phoning *01733 416477*.

By air

Norway is dotted with domestic airports, which makes travelling the often long distances more practical. **SAS** (*www.sas.no*), **Braathens** (*www.braathens.no*) and **Color Air** (*www.colorair.no*) all offer domestic flights to various points around the country.

By bus

A national network of express buses (*www.nor-way.no*) covers the entire country, and can be a comfortable and stress-free way of getting around. Tickets can be bought on board.

By train

The **NSB** (Norwegian State Railway) (*tel: (47) 81 50 08 88*) network is comprehensive in the south of the country, but ends in Bodø in northern Norway. However, there is also a system known as *Togbuss* ('train-bus'), which goes up as far north as Tromsø and the Lofoten Islands. If you are planning a lot of rail travel, the Norway Rail Pass, which offers fares at a 20 per cent discount, is worth buying. There are first- and second-class carriages on most Norwegian trains, but second class is clean and comfortable so the extra expenditure to upgrade isn't really worth

A village post office in Svalbard

Oslo transport network

Practical guide

it. In the fjord region, lines such as the Flåmsbana (*see p94*) have become tourist attractions in their own right.

Oslo transport

Oslo has an extensive network of metro lines (T-banen), trams and local railway lines covering the city.

By taxi

The easiest way to get a taxi in the cities is at a taxi rank, although you are allowed to hail one in the street if there isn't a rank nearby. Taxis are metered, and fares are standardised according to the time of day and the distance to be covered. To call a taxi by phone, dial 23 23 23 23, but note that the fare begins from the minute you make the call.

By ferry

The Hurtigruten ferries run between Bergen and Kirkenes (*see p27*) every day, with 34 ports of call along the coast. There are also a number of express ferries in the fjord region, and a wide range of car ferries.

Danger: reindeer crossing

Smoking

Since 2004, smoking has been banned in all public places, including bars, restaurants, nightclubs and on public transport. Smoking is permitted at outside tables of bars and restaurants.

Student travel

Students should carry an International Student Identity Card (ISIC), which will entitle them to valuable discounts on admission fees to sights, as well as on ferries and public transport.

Sustainable tourism

Thomas Cook is a strong advocate of ethical and fairly traded tourism and believes that the travel experience should be as good for the places visited as it is for the people that visit them. That's why we are a firm supporter of **The Travel Foundation**, a charity that develops solutions to help improve and protect holiday destinations, their environment, traditions and culture. To find out what you can do to make a positive difference to the places you travel to and the people who live there, please visit *www.thetravelfoundation.org.uk*

Taxes

All non-Scandinavian residents are entitled to claim back the 20 per cent tax added on to goods costing more than 310 Nkr at shops that display a 'tax-free goods' sign. You must present your passport and ask for a tax-free shopping form. When you leave the country, the form should be handed in to the Tax Free counter at your point of departure and a refund in kroner will be handed to you.

Telephones

There are both card and coin public phone boxes in public areas and at post offices. Pay phones accept 1, 5, 10 and 20 Nkr coins, and the cheapest rates can be had between 5pm and 8am during the week, and throughout the weekend. A *telekort* (phonecard) can be bought at post offices and kiosks. The country code for Norway is *47*. For directory enquiries, dial *180*. To call abroad from Norway, dial *00*, then the appropriate country code.

Australia *61*
Ireland *353*
New Zealand *64*
UK *44*
USA and Canada *1*

Time

Norway's time zone is GMT + 1 hour. The UK and Ireland are 1 hour behind, Australia and New Zealand are 9 hours ahead, and the USA and Canada are 6 hours and 9 hours behind on the east and west coasts respectively.

Tipping

Service charges are included in restaurant bills and taxi fares, so you do not have to add on any extra to what is likely to be, in foreigners' eyes, an already large amount. If you have had exceptional service, however, feel free to show your appreciation with a small tip. Taxi drivers will, however, expect a tip if they help you with a lot of heavy luggage.

Tourist offices

Australia *17 Hunter Street, Yarralumla, ACT 2600. Tel: (61) 2 6273 3444.*
Canada *2 Bloor St West, Suite 504, Toronto, Ontario M4W 3E2. Tel: (1) 416 920 0434.*
Ireland *27 Auburn Terrace, Donnybrook, Dublin 4. Tel: (353) 1 668 0333.*
UK *Charles House, 5 Regent Street, London SW1Y 4LR. Tel: (44) 020 7389 8800.*
USA *655 3rd Ave, Suite 1810, New York 10017. Tel: (01) 212 949 2333.*

Travellers with disabilities

Norway is relatively well equipped for travellers with disabilities. Most pavements have ramps, as do ferries, and road crossings are equipped with beeps to indicate when to cross for the sight impaired. **RADAR** (*www.radar.org.uk*), a UK-based organisation, sells, for a nominal fee, packs with detailed advice for travellers with disabilities abroad, while the Norway-specific **Norwegian Association of the Disabled** (*www.nhf.no*) offers valuable information.

Tourist Information Offices will provide all the help you require

Index

A
accommodation 172–7
Adventdalen 142
Agder-Naturmuseum &
Botaniske Hage 64
air travel 178, 185
Akershus Castle 30–31
Ålesund 19, 82–3, 170, 175
Alta 133–4
Åmot i Modum 44–5
Andøya 124
Archaeology, Museum of 73
archipelago cruises 63
architecture 19, 68
see also stave churches
Archive Centre 83
Arctic Cathedral 130
Arctic Circle 8, 114–15
Arendal 69
Art Museum of Northern
Norway 131–2
Art Nouveau Centre 83
Åseral 75
Astrup Fearnley Museum
of Modern Art 31
Atlantic Road 88–9
Atlantic Sea Park 83
Aust-Agder Museum 69
Austvågøy 117–18
Averøy 89

B
Balestrand 92
banks 184
Barentsburg 142–3
beaches 158
Bergen 4, 48–59, 148
accommodation 174–5
entertainment 154,
155–6, 157
restaurants 169–70
shopping 153
sights 48–59
Bergen Aquarium 54
Bergen Art Museum 52–3
Bergen Kunsthall 53
Bergen Maritime Museum
54
Bergen Museum 54
Bjarkøy 126
Bjørnøya 147
Bjørnson, Bjørnstjerne 21,
33, 35
Blood Road Museum 115
Bodø 111, 175
Borgund 96
Botanical Gardens,
Kristiansand 64
Botanical Gardens, Oslo
42–3
Botanical Gardens, Tromsø
130
Brekkeparken 77
Bremsnes Cave 89
Brønnøysund 111–12
Bryggen Gallery 50, 51
Bryggens Museum 50
Bu Museum, Ringøy 86, 87
Bud 89
Buekorps Museum 54–5
Bugøynes 134
Bull, Ole 20, 57, 58
buses, long-distance 178,
185
Bygdøy Peninsula 38–40
Byglandsfjorden 75

C
camping 173
canoeing 162
Canon Museum 64–5
car hire 179
central Norway 102–23
children 158–60
Christiansholm Fortress 63
climate and seasons 8, 26,
178–9
climbing 162–3
cobalt mines 44
cod-fishing industry 122–3
conversion table 181
cost of living 5, 29
costume, traditional 18, 81
credit cards 182, 184
crime 179
culture 18–21
customs regulations 179
cycling 163

D
Damsgård Manor 57
Danskøya 143
De Syv Søstre 116
Decorative Arts & Design,
Museum of 33
disabilities, travellers with
189
dog sledge trips 144–5, 148
Dombås 102
Dovrefjell National Park 9,
102–3, 151
Dovregubbens Rike
Trollpark 102
driving 28, 178, 179–80
Dyreparken 64, 160

E
Eidfjord 86, 87
Eidsvoll 45
electricity 181
Elverum 103
embassies and consulates
181
emergency telephone
numbers 181
entertainment 154–7
etiquette 28–9, 188
explorers 46–7

F
Fantoft Stave Church 57
Fauske 112
Femundsmarka National
Park 104
ferry services 27, 178, 187
festivals and events 22–5
Finnmark 4, 133–9
Fish Market, Bergen 55
fishing 163
Fiskebrygga Harbourfront
63
Fjærland 93
fjords 4, 6, 72, 75, 80–97,
150–51
Flakstadøy 119
Flåm 94, 175
Flåm Railway 28, 94
Fløibanen Funicular 55–6
flora and fauna 8–9, 151
Florø 94
food and drink 166–71
forests 8
Fossheim Steinsenter 106

Fram polar ship 38
Frammuseet 38
Fredrikstad 66
Fredriksten Fortress 67
Frogner Park 41

G
Galleri Bryggen 50, 51
Galleri Svalbard 145
Geilo 95
Geirangerfjord 83–4, 175
Giske 84
Gjenreisningsmuseet 135
Gjesværstappan 134
glaciers 6, 90–91, 164
golf 164
Gossen 84
Grand Café, Oslo 37
Grenseland Museum 137
Grieg, Edvard 20, 58, 59,
101
Grimstad 69–70
Grimstad Town Museum &
Ibsen House 70
Grønland 42
Gronligrotta 115
Gulatinget 95
Guovdageiannu Gilisillju
136

H
Hadeland Glassverk,
Jevnaker 45
Hadseløya 124
Håkon's Hall 49
Halden 67
Hamar 104
Hammerfest 134–5
Hamningberg 139
Hanseatic Assembly Rooms
50, 51
Hanseatic Museum 50, 51
Hardanger 8, 80–82
Hardanger Folk Museum
86–7
Harstad 126
Hattfjelldal 112
Haugesund 71, 176
Haugfoss 44
health 182
Heddal stave church,
Notodden 76
Hellesylt 85
Henningsvær 118
Herbarium 112
Heyerdahl, Thor 38, 46–7,
67
hiking 164
Hildurs Uterarium 112
Historical Museum 32
history 10–13
hitchhiking 28
Hjemmeluft Petroglyphs
133–4
Holmenkollen Ski Museum
42
Honningsøya 89
Hopen 147
horse riding 159–60, 164–5
hostels 173
hotels 172, 174–7
Hvaler 67

I
Ibsen, Henrik 21, 35, 37,
70, 77, 101

Ibsen Museum 32–3
Ice Skating Museum 41
insurance 180, 182
Internet access 182
Ishaavskatedralen 130

J
Josteldalsbreen National
Park 6, 90–91
Jotunheimen National Park
6, 96
Jugendstilsenteret 83

K
Karasjok 135, 170, 176
Karlsøy 126
Kautokeino 136
Kinsarvik 86
Kirkenes 136–7
Kjerringøy Trading Post
113–14
Kløckers House 69
Kon-Tiki Museum 38
Kongelige Slott 37
Kongsberg 75
Kongsberg Solvgruver 75–6
Kongsfjorden 143–4
Kragerø 69
Kråkenes Fyr 91
Kristiansand 60, 62–6, 170,
176
Kristiansand Zoo &
Amusement Park 64,
160
Kristiansund 89
Krossfjorden 144
Kunstindustrimuseet 33
Kvitøya 147

L
Lærdal 96, 176
Laksforsen Waterfall 113
landscape 6–9
Langøya 124–5
languages 18, 29, 183
Larvik 67
Leka 108
Leprosy Museum 56
Lille Lungegårdsvann 52–3
Lillehammer 27, 104–5,
170, 176
Lindesnes Lighthouse 70
Lofoten Islands 4, 117–23,
149–50, 170, 176
Lofoten Stockfish Museum
120
Lofoten Viking Museum 121
Lofthus 86
log cabins 158, 172
Lom 106
Longyearbyen 144
Lyngen Alps 126–7
Lyngenfjord 126–7
Lysefjord 72
Lysøen Island 57–8
Lysverket 53

M
Mack Brewery 131
Magdalenefjord 145–6
Magic Ice 119
Maihaugen Folk Museum
105
Målselvfossen Waterfall 127
Mandal 70
Mardalsfossen 85

Mariakirken 50, 51
Maritime Museum, Oslo 39–40
Maritime Museum, Stavanger 74
medical treatment 182
Merdø 69
Midnight Sun 129
Misvær 115
Mo i Rana 114
Moffen 146
Molde 88–9, 176
money 182, 184
Møre and Romsdal 82–5
Mosjøen 113, 177
Moskenesøy 119
mountain hut accommodation 173
Munch, Edvard 19–20, 35, 43, 70
Munch Museum 43
music 20–21, 156–7
Music History, Museum of 109

N
Nærøyfjord 96
Namsos 108
National Gallery 33–4
national holidays 184
National Museum of Contemporary Art 33
National Theatre 37
Nature Museum & Botanical Gardens 64
newspapers 182
Nidaros Cathedral 109
Nordaustandlet 147
Nordfjord 90–92
Nordfjord Folk Museum 91
Nordkapp 137–8, 177
Nordland 110–13
Nordnorsk Kunstmuseum 131–2
Nordre Venstøp 77
Norsk Barnemuseum 158–9
North Cape Maritime Museum 137–8
North Norwegian Preservation Centre and Boat Museum 126
Northern Lights 26, 128–9
Northern Lights Planetarium 131
northern Norway 124–39
Norway's Resistance Museum 34
Norwegian Aviation Museum 111
Norwegian Canning Museum 74
Norwegian Emigrant Museum 104
Norwegian Fisheries Museum 56
Norwegian Fishing Museum 119
Norwegian Fjord Centre 86
Norwegian Folk Museum 38–9
Norwegian Forestry Museum 103–4
Norwegian Glacier Museum 93–4
Norwegian Knitting Museum 58
Norwegian Maritime Museum 39–40

Norwegian Mining Museum 76
Norwegian Museum of Historic Vehicles 105
Norwegian Olympic Museum 106
Norwegian Petroleum Museum 73
Norwegian Railway Museum 104
Norwegian Wild Salmon Centre 96
Ny-Ålesund 146

O
Old Bergen Exchange 49
Old Bergen Museum 58
Olympic Park 105–6
opening hours 184
Oppdal 107
Ørnes 115
Oslo 4, 19, 30–43, 148
accommodation 174
entertainment 154–5, 156–7
restaurants 168–9
shopping 152–3
sights 30–43
transport network 186–7
Oslo Cathedral 36, 37
Oslo City Museum 41
Oslo University 37
Østfold & Vestfold 66–8
Our Saviour's Cemetery 35
Øvre Dividal National Park 127

P
Parliament Building 37
passports and visas 158, 178
Pasvik National Park 138
Pasvik Valley 138
Pasvikdalen 138
pharmacies 182, 184
polar bears 146, 180
Polar Museum 132
Polar Night 129
Polaria 132
Polarsirkelsenteret 115
police 181, 184
politics and economy 16–17
Pomor Museum 143
Posebyen 63
post offices 184
Postwar Reconstruction, Museum of 135
public transport 27–8, 184–7

R
Rago National Park 116
Ramsøya 89
Rasmus Meyer Collection 53
Raumabanen Railway 85
Ravenedalen Nature Park 65
Refsvikhula 120
Reisa National Park 127, 130
Ringve Musikkhistorisk Museum 109
Risør 71
Risør Aquarium 71
Roald Amundsen Centre 66
rock carvings and paintings 89, 90, 116–17, 133
Romsdal Museum 88, 89
Rondane National Park 107
Røros 107

Rosenkrantz Tower 49
Royal Blåfarveværk 44–5
Royal Palace 37
Ruija Kvenmuseum 138–9
Runde 87, 151

S
safaris 159
St Olav 108
Salten Museum, Bodø 111
Salten Museum, Rognan 115
Saltfjellet-Svartisen National Park 116
Saltstraumen 116
Sami Museum 135–6
Sami people 4, 18, 127, 135–6, 139
Sami Settlement Museum 136
Sami Theme Park 136
Sámiid Vuorká Dávvirat 135–6
Sandefjord 67–8
Sápmi 136
Schøtstuene 50, 51
scuba diving 165
Selje 92
Seljord 76
Setergrotta 115
Setesdalsbanen 76–7
Seven Sisters Range 116
shopping 152–3, 184, 188
Siljustøl 58–9
Silver Mines 75–6
Sjoa 107–8
Skåren 116
Skien 77
skiing 42, 78–9, 92, 95, 163–4, 165
Skøytemuseet 41
smoking etiquette 188
Sogn and Fjordan Coastal Museum 95
Sognefjord 6, 92–3, 150
Sørlandet Art Museum 62–3
southern Norway 60–77
Spangereid Vikingland 71
Spitsbergen 142–6
sport and leisure 159–60, 162–5
Stavanger 71, 72–4, 170–1, 177
Stavanger Museum 73–4
stave churches 19, 38, 57, 76, 96, 97, 98–9, 106, 108
Stenersen 53
Stiftsgården 109–10
Stiklestad 110
Stortinget 37
Storvågen 119
Stryn Summer Ski Centre 92
student travel 188
Sulitjelma Mining Museum 116
Sunnmøre 85
Sunnmøre Museum 83
Svalbard 8, 9, 27, 142–7, 150, 180
Svalbard Museum 145
Sverresborg Trøndelag Folkemuseum 110
Svolvær 118–19

T
tax-free shopping 188
taxis 187
Telemark 74–7

Telemark Canal 77, 151
telephones 188
television 182
theatre and literature 21, 157
Theatre Museum 35
theme parks and funfairs 160
Theodor Kittelsen Museum 45
Theta Museum 50, 51
time differences 189
Tingvoll 89
tipping 189
Tønsberg 68
Torghatten Peak 113
tourist information 189
tours, organised 184
Town Hall, Oslo 34–5
train services 178, 185, 187
trains, steam 76–7, 85
Tro 116–17
Troldhaugen 59
Troll Park 130
trolls and other myths 4, 100–1, 102, 130
Trollstigen 85
Troms 126–7, 130–33
Tromsø 4, 8, 130–33, 171, 177
Tromsø Defence Museum 132–3
Tromsø Museum 132
Trøndelag 108–10
Trøndelag Folk Museum 110
Trondheim 108–9, 171, 177
tundra 8

U
Ulriksbanen 56
Ulvik 87
Urnes 96–7

V
Vadsø 138–9, 171, 177
Værøy 120
Vågå 108
Vår Frelsers Gravlund 35
Varanger Sami Museum 139
Varangerbotn 139
Vardø 139
Várjjat Sámi Musea 139
Vega 138–9
Vesterålen Islands 124–5, 150
Vestfold Folk Museum 68
Vestvågøy 121
Vigeland House Museum 70
Vigeland Museum 41–2
Vigeland Park 20, 42
Vikøyri 97
Viking Land 45, 160
Viking Ship Museum 40
Vikings 4, 10, 14–15
Vingen 90
Vøringfossen Waterfall 83
Voss 27, 81, 177
Voss Folk Museum 82

W
War Memorial Museum 119
West Agder Folk Museum 65–6
West Norway Museum of Decorative Art 53
whale-watching 118, 124, 141
whaling 140–41
white-water rafting 107–8, 165
winter sports 78–9, 165

Acknowledgements

Thomas Cook Publishing wishes to thanks TERJE RAKKE, NORDIC LIFE for the photographs in this book, to whom the copyright belongs (except for the following).

DREAMSTIME 121 (Daniel Kristensen)
FLICKR 21 (Jesús Corrius); 25 (Frank K); 79 (Kalev Kevad); 82 (Dennis Wright); 84 (color line); 91, 93 (Thomas Mues); 118 (m.prinke); 140 (Erwin Winkelman); 144 (Geir Arne Brevik); 160 (Paal Leveraas)
JACQUELINE FRYD 17, 20, 24, 26, 28, 33, 35, 39, 40, 41, 43, 55, 56, 61, 64, 65, 69, 77, 78, 94, 97, 105, 106, 109, 110, 112, 113, 153, 155, 156, 157, 162, 163, 164, 165, 166, 168, 171, 173, 188
ROBERT HARDING 23
TORFINN JAERNET, NORDIC LIFE 66, 137, 143, 147
WIKIMEDIA 22 (Rafal Konieczny); 111 (Røed); 120 (Zorrolll); 134 (Andreas Rümpel); 136 (Yan Zhang)
WORLD PICTURES/PHOTOSHOT 1, 138

For CAMBRIDGE PUBLISHING MANAGEMENT LTD
Project editor: Lisa Firth
Proofreader: Jan McCann
Indexer: Marie Lorimer
Typesetter: Julie Crane

SEND YOUR THOUGHTS TO
BOOKS@THOMASCOOK.COM

We're committed to providing the very best up-to-date information in our travel guides and constantly strive to make them as useful as they can be. You can help us to improve future editions by letting us have your feedback. If you've made a wonderful discovery on your travels that we don't already feature, if you'd like to inform us about recent changes to anything that we do include, or if you simply want to let us know your thoughts about this guidebook and how we can make it even better – we'd love to hear from you.

Send us ideas, discoveries and recommendations today and then look out for your valuable input in the next edition of this title.

Emails to the above address, or letters to Travellers Series Editor, Thomas Cook Publishing, PO Box 227, Coningsby Road, Peterborough PE3 8SB, UK.

Please don't forget to let us know which title your feedback refers to!